Information at Work

Trade Union Industrial Studies

This series makes two new types of provision in the area of industrial relations: first it is specifically directed to the needs of active trade unionists who want to equip themselves to be more effective, and second, the books are linked together in a series related to the requirements of existing training and education courses.

The books have been designed by a Curriculum Development Group drawn from the Society of Industrial Tutors: Michael Barratt Brown, Ed Coker, Jim Fyrth, Bob Houlton and Geoffrey Stuttard, together with Charles Clark and Francis Bennett of the Hutchinson Publishing Group. The Curriculum Development Group has prepared the guide lines for the texts and edited them so that they form a complete set of teaching material for tutors and students primarily for use on trade union courses.

The texts are issued in sets of four, together with an accompanying resource book which provides additional background material for tutors and students.

Trade Union Industrial Studies

This series is published in three sets, each consisting of four student texts and an accompanying resource book. This book includes additional teaching material for tutors and students, a recommended list of books and a further exploration of the subjects by the authors of the texts.

The Activist's Handbook *Bob Houlton*
Statistics for Bargainers *Karl Hedderwick*
Calculating *Joyce & Bill Hutton*
The Organized Worker *Tony Topham*
Industrial Studies 1: the key skills
Eds. Ed Coker & Geoffrey Stuttard

Industrial Action *Ernie Johnston*
Pay at Work *Bill Conboy*
Work Study *Jim Powell*
Workers' Rights *Paul O'Higgins*
Industrial Studies 2: the bargaining context
Eds. Ed Coker & Geoffrey Stuttard

The Union Rule Book *Richard Fletcher*
Information at Work *Michael Barratt Brown*
Trade Unions and Government *Ann Taylor*
Industrial Studies 3: understanding industrial society
Eds. Ed Coker & Geoffrey Stuttard

Michael Barratt Brown

Information at Work

Arrow Books
in association with the Society
of Industrial Tutors

In memory of Bill Hutton, who tried hard to teach me the elements of accounting and who died in the middle of correcting the first draft of this book. Without his help and without the criticisms of the members of the Curriculum Development Group of the Hutchinson Arrow Books Trade Union Industrial Studies Series, and particularly those of Bob Houlton, this book would be even less easy for trade union activists to use. As it is, I hope that it will meet their needs; for the future of British industry lies in their hands.

Arrow Books Limited
3 Fitzroy Square, London W1P 6JD

An imprint of the Hutchinson Publishing Group

London Melbourne Sydney Auckland
Wellington Johannesburg and agencies
throughout the world

First published 1978

Set in Monotype Times
Made and printed in Great Britain
by The Anchor Press Ltd
Tiptree, Essex

ISBN 0 09 915920 1

Contents

Note: the first time that a word is used that may have a special meaning in accounting it is set in SMALL CAPITALS and you can look it up in the Glossary.

Photographic acknowledgements

Photographs have been reproduced by courtesy of:

HMSO: page 28
Arthur Foster Camera Press London: page 62
Sheffield Morning Telegraph: page 73
Extel Statistical Services Ltd: page 77
Camera Press: page 82
Henry Grant: page 95
TOPIX: page 106
General Electric Company: page 111

Part I: What There is to Know

Introduction: What is the Value of Information?

We would not accept facts and figures at face value. They [the management] had to produce them to our satisfaction and justify them. We broke down the whole process of manufacture into its constituent processes and sought the best solutions. We acquired a great deal of knowledge about production and because of that were able to make informed decisions. . . . I don't see participation as the be-all and end-all but a step into the future. It is a process of involving more and more people in the process of management. By acquiring that knowledge we are able to challenge them and more than that we would be able to run the system should the need arise. (Derek Robinson, Trade Union representative on the Leyland Car Council, talking about the Participation Committees at Leyland Motors to Arthur Smith of the *Financial Times,* 15 October 1976).

If you're on the inside, then you're in the know. It doesn't matter whether it's horse racing, the stock exchange, company investment or any other form of gambling. It doesn't mean you'll get it right, but you'll have all that a good INFORMATION SYSTEM can give you. In fact, whatever organization you work for, you are on the inside and at least partly in the know.

You may work for a company or a board or a local authority or a department of state. At your place of work you receive instructions down the line about the work you are expected to do, and how it relates to the work of others. You may be paid at the rate that the union has negotiated for your grade of work, with or without bonus and overtime. Payment may be made weekly or monthly with deductions for your liability to tax, insurance, wage-related superannuation, etc., along with hundreds or even thousands of others for whom the computer churns out the pay slips. You are part of a complex network of relationships, which depends upon the communication of facts and figures about what is to be done, where, when, in what way, and then upon what has been done and the payments that must be made.

Any organization, whether it is a company or state corporation

or public authority, has a vast information system. Some of the bits of the system you may know intimately. Other bits will be quite unknown to you. If you want to know more, you can find out a lot just by asking questions: about how information is collected and passed on in calculating your pay, for example, or in ordering equipment and supplies for use where you work, about the way decisions are made that affect you. This will lead you to asking who makes them, at different levels and in different parts of the organization.

Sooner or later you will have to set down what you have learned systematically. You can use all sorts of fancy devices. Some of these have names: ORGANIZATION TREES, with ladders and branches, diagrams of PRODUCT FLOWS, MULTIPLE ACTIVITY CHARTS, STOCK RECORDS, INPUT and OUTPUT balances, PERFORMANCE INDICATORS and financial ACCOUNTS The organization and methods experts have given special names to these ways of describing different parts of the system. You don't need to be frightened of the names; they are not really mysterious, just a form of shorthand.

The aim of this book is to help you to find your way through the great mass of information that you can quite easily collect yourself about the organization and finance of your work, and then to suggest how you may supplement this with information that is not so readily accessible. The main thing to remember is that information is not of any special value for its own sake. You can go on collecting more and more facts and figures; but if you don't know how to connect and compare them, how to make them reveal the real underlying relationships of people and the movements of goods and of money, then they are as useless as the random letters and figures a monkey might produce from a typewriter.

This is especially true of information given in numbers. It means little or nothing unless it is set out under headings and the units of measurement – £ or £millions (£m), or tonnes or million tonnes, etc. – are made clear, as well as the period or periods of time to which the figures relate.

To sum up: to use information effectively, you will have to decide:

What you want the information for?
What policy you are pursuing that requires it?
In what detail you want it.
For what period of time?
At what level of plant, division and company?
Who is going to use it at different levels of your own union organizations?

1. Why Keep Accounts?

Family Accounts

The most difficult kind of information may seem to you to be the financial accounts, so we shall begin with them. Most families in Britain are very good at managing their money. You will almost certainly have kept accounts at one time or another, for your own purposes or for your family household. You may even have kept accounts for a club or other joint activity. You probably decided to list sources of income on one page and items of expenditure on another. If you tried to compare one year with another in your household accounts, you may have grouped the items into categories, like rent and house repairs, food, clothing and footwear, travel, drink, tobacco, etc. Let us start, then, with an example from the Family Expenditure Survey which is made each year by the Department of Employment from a sample of about 10000 families in the United Kingdom.

If we take just those families consisting of a man and wife and two children, we find in the 1975 Survey that each family had on average $1\frac{1}{2}$ incomes. Let us call this a man's full-time and wife's part-time earnings. The figures are adjusted to give us a weekly sum for income and expenditure although some items will only be bought once in a year and their cost has to be averaged over the 52 weeks. Even so, in fact, the figures show an excess of expenditure over income. That won't surprise anyone! Borrowings and CREDIT received are not shown, but they are important parts of most people's accounts nowadays. Here, then, is a summary statement of the weekly income and expenditure of our average family of four in 1975:

Table 1: Income and Expenditure per Week of Family of Four, UK, 1975 (£)

Gross income of family	Wages and salaries	70·91	
	Other income	12·67	
			83·58
Deductions	Income tax	13·70	
	NI contributions	3·28	
			16·98
Net income			66·60
Current expenditure		69·29	
Pensions contributions, savings, etc.		4·58	
			73·87
Excess of outgoings over net income			7·27

Table 2: Details of Weekly Expenditure of Man, Wife and Two Children Family, UK, 1975 (£)

Housing, including rates (half the families owned or were buying their own house)			12·43
Repairs and decorations, etc.			1·32
Fuel, light and power (one half on electricity)			3·51
Food, of which	Bread, biscuits, cereals	1·99	
	Meat, poultry, fish	4·11	
	Dairy produce, cheese, eggs	2·69	
	Meals out	2·23	
	Other	5·43	
			16·45
Drink			2·80
Tobacco			2·07
Household goods – Durable			4·98
– Other			4·86
Clothing and footwear (about a third for children)			5·46
Transport (over 80% had a car)			9·51
Services (a third on holidays)			5·40
Pocket money, etc.			0·50
Total			69·29

SOURCE: Department of Employment, *Family Expenditure Survey, 1975*

This last set of figures simply states the outgoings, but you might want to look at some of them in a more analytical way, that is by breaking them down a bit more. We will take two examples, house ownership and the use of a car, for they illustrate many of the points that we shall be exploring in this book. Take the payments on the house: most of the families surveyed were buying their own houses, and making regular payments to a building society. These payments could just be thought of as RENT, but for the fact that a house is a CAPITAL ASSET, that is to say that an income can be obtained from letting it and it has a certain value in the MARKET. And you can raise a MORTGAGE on a house. That means that you can borrow the money to pay for the house, and deposit the DEEDS of the house with the BUILDING SOCIETY or BANK that lends you the money. The house needs repairs and maintenance, but when the payments are complete, it is the owner's property, and won't be a pile of rubble for a few years yet. A man and wife owning a house would still have to include IMPUTED RENT in their expenditure for the survey, that is what they could charge for letting the house, or what they would have to pay if they were renting it. Even before payments are complete, they can sell up and the payments already made can be transferred through the building society to another house. So a capital value may be set on the house, according to the market prices prevailing and the payments already made.

Take next the ownership and use of a car. A figure is given in the table corresponding to a weekly payment for the purchase of the car as well as a figure for maintenance and RUNNING COSTS. The car may have been bought on HP. Then the cost (in £) could be, for example:

	£
(List Price of Car	1000)
Down payment	150
Twelve monthly payments of	
£100 per month	1200
Total payments	1350
Weekly payments over one year	26

But this is much too much, because, of course, the owner still has the car, which he can presumably sell. He won't of course expect to get the original list price, because the car will have depreciated with use. What he should add to the costs of petrol, licensing and maintenance is a figure for DEPRECIATION. At the end of one year the car will be worth, say, £750 and after three years it may only be worth £400. The real cost over one year, therefore, is £1350 minus £750, that is, £600. This figure divided by 52 weeks would come to £11·54 per week. Over three years the sum would be £950 divided by 156 weeks, that is, £6·09 per week. The owner can use the trade-in value of the car to make a down payment on a new or newer car and can start on a new hire purchase.

Most businessmen would want to avoid paying such a high rate of interest as £350 on a £1000 car, that is 35 per cent per year, and would set money aside to cover depreciation. Thus, if the car depreciated by £600 in three years, as in our example, they would reckon this at £600 divided by 156 weeks, that is, £3·85 per week. In a period of rising prices, that might not be enough to ACCUMULATE towards buying a new car of the same sort, but they could reckon on lending the money they were setting aside and getting some interest on it to help. We are beginning to see that we need to make a careful distinction between *capital* accounts, covering the purchase and sale and depreciation of capital assets, and CURRENT accounts which are made up of the day-to-day receipts and expenses of a household or business. Over the years it is important to maintain this distinction. Otherwise you will find yourself suddenly faced with a large capital outlay, whether for a car or for the house, and no income to meet it.

Buisness Accounts for a Shopkeeper, Self-employed

Here is a story about a man who had to start keeping accounts when he became self-employed. Jim took his redundancy money which came to about £3000 and bought a shop. In fact the shop cost nearer £10000 but he found a bank that would take him as a customer and accept a mortgage on the shop for a LOAN of £7000. There were some fixtures like a deep-freeze in the shop and some unsold stock thrown in. He and his family moved in above the shop. They had some SAVINGS which they put into doing the place up and paying CASH down for certain goods. The rest they got on credit of one month, two months, three months, according to the WHOLESALERS' terms. At first it seemed to be all paying out; but as SALES increased, things got a bit easier and after six months Jim realized that he was beginning to make money. He started taking sums out of the business as wages for himself and stopped having to run down his savings. The value of his sales was exceeding his EXPENDITURE, including outgoings on the bank loan, RATES, the electricity bill, VAT, and so on. But he knew that he had some outstanding accounts to settle and there was the money he'd put into stock. At the same time there were customers who had run up DEBTS, most of which he was pretty sure would be repaid. But he knew there would be some BAD DEBTS. He tried working out a BALANCE of all these sums for the six months' period, but realized that this would involve a STOCKTAKING to check what he actually had in stock that was really saleable compared with what he'd started with. He put this off to the end of the year, but he knew he'd have to do it then.

After a year Jim sat down to work out just what his EARNINGS were, that is after deducting all costs from his sales. He had to do this for the tax inspector. He worked out the value of the stock he started with and the value he finished with after WRITING OFF unsaleable items. He knew the value of what he had bought in and he knew the value of his sales. He had some outstanding payments on credit and some debts due. There were some costs he was unsure about, for example, the use of the van which he'd had when he started up and which was used mostly for deliveries and collections but also for family outings. Then there was the telephone that was mainly, but not wholly, used for business. He had a separate electricity account for the shop, so that wasn't a problem. But what about his wife's part-time work in the shop? How should he charge that? And there were his insurance stamps as a self-employed person. Presumably they could be charged as costs. All these things had to go down on Schedule D of the tax return in which costs can be set against GROSS INCOME before NET INCOME is arrived at. (If you're on a wage or salary you pay tax on Schedule E, generally as PAYE.) But what should he do about his own wages? Jim realized that he'd better get some help from an accountant. One of the questions the accountant asked was about depreciation on the van, on equipment, and on the building itself. It was only when all these things were taken into account that Jim really knew what his earnings were over the year. He was rather pleased to find that they were rather more than he'd paid out to himself as wages, but he had plans for new equipment, a new van and an extension to the shop. Although the accountant said that these could be capital costs, Jim knew he'd have to find them out of his earnings if he wasn't going to borrow more money. So he put some money aside, into what the accountant called a RESERVE fund.

Jim's accounts probably looked like this at the end of the year:

Table 3: Jim's Accounts (£)

1. Capital account			
Capital at beginning of year		to *Assets* at beginning of year	
Redundancy money	3000	Shop, fixtures	10000
Bank loan	7000	Improvements	500
Savings, etc.	1000	Van	500
2. Current account over the year			
Income, credit		*Expenditure*	
From sales	20000	Stock at cost	12000
Less debts	1000	*Less* credit	2000
Total	19000	Total	10000
Plus unsold stocks	1500	Rates	200
Less stocks written off	500	Gas, electricity, phone, etc.	500
		Interest to bank	1000
	1000	Petrol, etc.	300
Total	20000	Stamps, etc.	150
		Depreciation	500
		Miscellaneous	350
			3000
Balance	7000	Total	13000
To tax	2500		
To wages for self, wife	4000		
To reserve fund	500		

Note that Jim had received more credit (£2000) than he had given (£1000). He is OK so long as his creditors don't foreclose on him suddenly; and he hopes he has no bad debts.

Business Accounts for Employers

An employer who runs a business and employs labour will want to see the accounts for many of the same reasons as a self-employed shopkeeper like Jim. However, unlike the self-employed, he can't know all that's going on in the business. He has sunk money in buildings, plant and equipment, and he will want to know not only the income but the current value of his capital, that is its worth after depreciation and after profits and losses. If there are several plants or several lines of production, he will want to know which ones are making the most PROFIT and which are making a loss. If he is an owner but leaves the running of the business to a BOARD of DIRECTORS and management, he may be content with that amount of knowledge. But directors and management will need to know much more:

Detailed costs of labour, materials, and so on, for each UNIT of output, for each product, for each plant, for each machine;
Regular sales returns for each product;
The stocks being carried;
Progress of new building and of other new INVESTMENTS;
The size of OVERDRAFTS, current debts and credit;
Cash in the bank;
Dates when bills are due and payments expected.

This kind of information will not be made available to all the owners if there are a large number, as in the case of the SHAREHOLDERS of a COMPANY; for that would make it public knowledge for COMPETITORS to use in their activities, or for trade unions to use in negotiations. It will certainly not generally be made available to the employees. They might use it for their own rather than for the company's advantage! The annual REPORT and ACCOUNTS of any business reveal no more than they have to – one aspect only of an information system that provides management with its eyes and ears.

But this is where workers have an enormous advantage in understanding the basis of the whole accounting system, especially trade union representatives who pick up information from workers in different departments and plants.

You may not be able to put the exact money tag on every item, but you will know:

Some of the costings; and what goes into making a product, the time spent, the materials used;
What's going into and out of stock;
What's selling and what isn't;
What ought to be replaced as well as what is being replaced;
How old the machinery is and how well new plant is working.

The weakness of this sort of information is that it is bitty; there are pieces missing. There isn't an overall view. That's what accounts and information systems are for.

We shall sum this chapter up with a basic business accounting model to look at. We shall be working at models like this in later chapters. This one is included here to sum up what we've been talking about in this chapter. Give it a preliminary run-through and think about the various listed items as they appear in the company, enterprise or office where you work. You won't be able to put figures to the items but you probably know much more about them than you thought you did at first.

If you were to insert figures against the items in the table overleaf, then income and profit (or loss) will be found by subtracting the total of the items in no. 1 from the total of the items in no. 4. Note that the items in no. 4 equal the total of the items in no. 3 subtracted from the total of the items in nos. 1 and 2.

Table 4: A Basic Business Accounting Model for a Period of Time (e.g. One Year) with Some Details Listed

1. Starting value of business at beginning of period represented by:	Buildings Plant Machinery and equipment	after depreciation
	Vehicles Stocks Work in progress Cash Credits less debts	
2. Receipts from	Sales of products, services home production home sales exports overseas production Interest on loans Other income (rents, etc.) Grants from Government	
3. Expenditure on:	Materials, fuel, power, after adjusting for stock movements Other bought-in products and services Rent Wages, salaries for labour Using up plant, machinery Interest on borrowing Taxation	
4. Finishing value of business at end of period represented by:	Buildings Plant Machinery, equipment	after depreciation
	Vehicles Stocks Work in progress Cash Credits less debts	

2. What You Know and They Don't: The Worm's Eye View

This isn't going to be a chapter about fiddles and skiving and petty thefts, although it well could be! What you know and they don't is not just a worm's eye view either. It's about the real effort involved in getting some jobs done; the real difficulties with certain machines; the real waste of time when supplies don't arrive, the wrong materials are delivered, parts don't fit; the real inefficiency of much industrial and commercial organization; the real loss of quality when priming is skimped, shoddy materials are used, inspection is lax. You name it; you know it. You wouldn't do it yourself like that; you'd have more sense. Yorkshire miners have a regular saying: 'We could manage t'bloody pit better oursen.' It is not just an arrogant boast; *you* know at *your* work-place. And the management often doesn't have a clue, especially at board level.

So much knowledge on the shop floor is of no interest to managers, if they cannot use it *and* control it. In the next chapter we shall look at management's information and control systems. Here we must notice one central aspect of industrial and commercial organization. This is the DIVISION OF LABOUR, which has the greatest possible effect on the view any worker has of his place in the whole organization he belongs to. It may seem quite obvious that labour should be divided up into the detailed jobs that you do and that you see being done all around you. The machines that you work with require minding, require maintenance at certain points, require driving or other forms of operation. But, of course, the machines were designed this way.

Let us listen for a minute to the father of 'scientific management', F. W. Taylor, writing a hundred years ago. Taylor worked at the Midvale Steel Company of Philadelphia, USA, and then at the giant Bethlehem Steel Company. His name is generally associated with the stop-watch, and he was called 'Speedy' Taylor; but much more important than the stop-watch, he introduced to these companies what he called a 'clear-cut and novel division of mental and manual labour throughout the workshops'. As a junior member of management Taylor 'fully realized' that, in his own words, 'although he was a foreman of the shop, the combined knowledge and skill of the workmen who were under him was at least ten times as great as his own'. He had no control over their output. When he tried to set higher NORMS they 'soldiered'. He determined then that the work process should be divided up and, as he put it, 'all possible brainwork would be removed from the shop and centred in the planning or layout department'. You will see that this was not only to increase production by having one man do one job. It was also intended, deliberately, to remove 'control' as much as possible from the workers and make it a management function. The reason why your knowledge is so often ignored is that if management gave it proper attention you would be likely to gain more shop-floor control.

During the last twenty years the controls that many factory- and mine-workers had over the pace and rhythm of their work have been destroyed by mechanization moving towards automation; and the knowledge and experience of many clerical workers have been replaced by the computer. In a book entitled *The Black-Coated Worker* (Cambridge, 1958), David Lockwood has written:

> One of the main changes in the division of labour has been the appearance of the specialised, semi-skilled office employee who is responsible for the 'processing' of data. The actual division of tasks very often preceded mechanisation, but machinery has speeded up the trend by which a small number of executives, who make decisions about the selection and analysis of data, are separated from a mass of subordinates whose functions less and less justify their classification as brain workers.

At first sight it might seem as if they've got you as morons; and there is little you can do about it. This book is designed to help you prove them wrong.

Workers in factories and offices still have brains, and rather better educated ones than before. One result of reducing the skill and responsibility of the clerical worker has been the enormous growth in white-collar unions. What divides them from manual workers has been greatly reduced. But Taylor's dream has never been wholly realized. The division of labour has only in a very few cases actually made workers into isolated atoms, content, so long as they are well paid, to revolve as individual parts of a machine they cannot control. Much work in factories and offices is in groups, and these groups *can* operate some joint controls through their trade union organization over what work they do and how they do it. And, which is what concerns us here, they come to possess over the years a great store of knowledge of the processes they are engaged on and the way that their organization functions. The fact that this knowledge is never called upon by management, except perhaps in a crisis like the three-day week in the winter of 1973–4, does not mean that it isn't of value. In the studies we shall be engaged upon in this book, this knowledge will be found to be invaluable.

Let us spell out some of the key factors of a business that any worker knows or can easily get to know.

Is the Plant Up-to-date or Clapped Out?

Here the information is concerned with the machinery, equipment and vehicles you work with: their cost, their age, CAPACITY and performance, output per day, per hour, etc., comparisons with older or more recent models, maintenance requirements, need for replacement parts, etc. One of the key questions in accounting we shall come to is the FINANCE of depreciation, that is of the wear and tear of plant, equipment and vehicles. You will know whether management is nursing a machine along or running it into the ground. What you have to think about is why it pays to do one or the other.

How Much Do They Buy In from Outside?

This is to do with fuel, power, raw materials and other bought-in items: what are the quantities and costs per hour or per unit of output, cost of rejects and of wasted or idle time? Stewards will know about 'down time' and the reasons for it: generally managerial inefficiency, and only rarely disputes. How much does your work depend on outside suppliers, sub-contractors, or on other plants of the same company or group at home or abroad? Are outside contractors doing work that could well be done in your own workshops? What about all the many interconnections that may reveal themselves to store men, truck drivers, tally clerks? We shall see later that a key concept for trade union negotiators is that of VALUE ADDED, that is the value added by the work done in one plant or one company or group to the materials, fuel and other supplies bought in. This, of course, is the work you do and you'll know of cases where some of it has been taken away and contracted out.

What are Labour Costs?

Labour costs are the measurements per unit of output. These will be of three kinds: (a) labour on the machine itself; (b) other DIRECT LABOUR in works, pit or transport, etc; (c) INDIRECT LABOUR in administration, supervision, office and headquarters staff, etc. Leyland stewards, for example, have accurate estimates of direct labour costs based on cars produced and workers on the line at fixed rates of pay; but it is not easy to allocate indirect labour costs. Increases in the proportion of supervisory staff to direct labour will be very obvious to workers. Have you never said, 'There's more bloody chiefs than Indians in this place?' The main point to look for in the accounts will be the proportion of value added that goes to wages and salaries on the one hand and that which goes to SURPLUS or forms of profit on the other.

Is the Stuff Getting Away?

Here we're talking about sales and stocks. The state of the order books, short-time or overtime working, delays in delivery, the stocks of materials being carried, the build-up or run-down of stocks of finished products are all telltale indicators of the state of business and of PROFITABILITY or threatened BANKRUPTCY. It's not much good going for a pay rise when the yard is full of unsold stuff. This is what is involved when there is talk about cash flow problems: too much cash flowing out and not enough coming in without borrowing more money to tide the business over, and paying a high rate of interest for it.

How They Fix the Prices

There are prices for FINAL PRODUCTS and SERVICES and for INTERMEDIATE PRODUCTS, that is, those that go into making something else, especially the TRANSFER PRICES of products or services from one department or plant or company to another in the same group; in MULTINATIONAL COMPANIES, that is those which operate in several countries, these transfer prices can be deliberately adjusted to bring losses in one place where taxes are high and profits in another where taxes are low. There are also DISCOUNTS, LOSS LEADERS and CROSS SUBSIDIES. It's hard to know what the value is of what you make.

Who Really Owns the Place?

Here what is involved are: the ultimate ownership of companies and plants and the links with other companies, family holdings and chief shareholders. You may know, for instance, of 'sleeping partners', members of the owner's family working in the company; connections with banks and INSURANCE COMPANIES – the backroom financiers – and with former government ministers on the board of directors. Below that there is the line of command down from the board of directors and managing director; and the status of staff managers like the personnel manager and research officer. You may know a bit about how management is recruited. There may be decentralization of profit-making centres in the company or group, you may know the names of outside consultants and accountants employed. This information will suggest where the sources of finance for the business are to be found and where the real power in the business lies.

Now, of course, it is very unlikely that you will be able to gather more than bits and pieces of all the information listed here without getting hold of a good deal of management's secret material; but most of it *can* be discovered from published material, as we shall see. The point of our list was to suggest the things you *can* find out for yourselves or already know. As with the accounting model you can run through the list again and you'll probably be surprised how much you and other trade union representatives already know.

3. What They Know and You Don't: The Information System

In China the ruling class of mandarins used to write official documents in a script that was so complicated it took twenty years of special schooling to master. In England entry to the top schools like Eton, Harrow, Rugby and Charterhouse used to depend on the ability at the age of twelve to write Latin and Greek verse. In 1960 one-third of the top company directors in finance and industry in Britain had been at Eton. Here is something this author wrote on an earlier occasion after a careful study of the controllers of British industry:*

Every governing class in history has tried to clothe the business of government in mystery, and the clerks who carried on the actual business have always resorted to magic words and signs to blind the ignorant. It is not for nothing that the most representative organization of British businessmen and financiers is the Secret Society of Freemasons. There are indeed some real secrets in business – the technical know-how and experience of firms (not of course patents, which by their very name imply that they are open but protected by law from theft). Most of the secrets, however, have nothing to do with competition but everything to do with confusing the uninformed worker. They are useful not only for concealing profits but also for concealing managerial inefficiency. This should not be taken to imply that secrets relating to competition are permissible. Secrecy about plans for a new product may lead to wasteful investment elsewhere. (From Michael Barratt Brown, *Opening the Books*, Institute for Workers Control, 1968, pp.1–2.)

So how much can you get to know without secrets being revealed? Overall figures for a group or company's sales, its profits, total employment and other information listed at the end of this chapter have to be published by law under the Companies Acts.

*'Who Controls British Industry?' in K. Coates (ed.), *Can the Workers Run Industry?* (Sphere Books, 1968)

The figures for sales and profits must be broken down by the main divisions and main national areas in a multi-product or multinational company. Separate accounts must be drawn up for the PARENT COMPANY and for the group as a whole, that is, including the SUBSIDIARIES at home or overseas and any associated companies. The value of exports from the UK must also be shown. Some companies show overall figures for value added in relation to materials, fuel and power and other bought-in products and services. All of the information which has by law to be supplied to shareholders is in effect public knowledge, since it is possible to go to COMPANIES HOUSE and get copies of any company's Annual Report and Accounts which is provided for its shareholders. Your company should provide these for all trade union representatives.

Secret Information

And what are the secrets? This is what the employers say:

'Employees should be *informed* about some important aspects of company policy; management should *consult* workers on matters which *management* consider directly affect them such as redundancies' (author's italics for emphasis), but 'essential facts of the company's business performance . . . are obviously not matters for consultation . . . ' (Engineering Employers' Federation Policy Paper, *Employee Participation*, EEF, 1974).

The kind of information disclosed to workers should be strictly limited by 'constraints arising out of competitive requirements and confidentiality. . . . Those whose disclosure would be too commercially sensitive include mergers and take-overs, investment and expansion; closures and changes in location; research and development; product changes; production schedules; savings resulting from increased productivity, and labour costs per unit of output.' (CBI, *The Provision of Information to Employees*, CBI, 1975.)

Under the Employment Protection Act 1975, the duty is laid on employers to disclose certain items of information to representatives of trade unions, as is seen in the figure here. The Act lists some exceptions:

1. Information such as might come under the Official Secrets Act where disclosure would be against the national interest.

Employment Protection Act 1975 c. 71 15

relating to his undertaking as is in his possession, or that of any associated employer, and is both— PART I

(*a*) information without which the trade union representatives would be to a material extent impeded in carrying on with him such collective bargaining, and

(*b*) information which it would be in accordance with good industrial relations practice that he should disclose to them for the purposes of collective bargaining.

(2) The collective bargaining for the purposes of which an employer must disclose information under subsection (1) above is collective bargaining about matters, and in relation to descriptions of workers,—

(*a*) in respect of which the trade union is recognised by that employer ; or

(*b*) falling within the scope of an operative recommendation for recognition (within the meaning of section 15 above) relating to the union,

and in this section and sections 19 to 21 below " representative ", in relation to a trade union, means an official or other person authorised by the trade union to carry on such collective bargaining.

2. Information communicated to the company in confidence.

3. Information relating specifically to an individual, unless he has consented to its being disclosed.

4. Information which would cause substantial injury to the undertaking for reasons other than its effect on collective bargaining. This is a very general exception, you can see, that might cover:

(a) Information about processes and technology which would be of value to a competitor.

(b) Information about financial affairs that might damage the reputation and standing of a business and encourage SPECULATION.

(c) Details of costs and profits for individual plants and for locations of activity where revelation might encourage workers to raise wage demands or alternatively cause undue alarm and despondency, or arouse local or national resentment.

5. Inspection or copying of documents other than those prepared for the purpose.

6. Compiling information which would involve an expenditure out of reasonable proportion to the value of the information in the conduct of collective bargaining.

The ACAS Code of Practice on Information Disclosure issued under the Employment Protection Act lists examples of information which could be relevant in certain bargaining situations:

Pay: principles and structure by either work group, grade, plant, sex, department or company;
Conditions of service: recruitment, training, promotion, redundancy, changes in work method, job evaluation, pension;
Employment: numbers by grades, departments, location, age, overtime;
Productivity: savings, shares of market, return on capital invested;
Finance: cost structures, transfer prices, parent company loans.

The Code of Practice is available from ACAS, Cleland House, Page Street, London SW1, and should be in every shop steward's possession.

A business that has a secret process has a monopoly which it can exploit by charging a high price. For this reason there is a vast amount of industrial spying, and not only between countries. Now it is just these secrets that you will know a lot about anyway. You may, for example, be working on a new process; but apart from the fact that you've probably signed a mouth-shutting clause in your contract, why should you be any less discreet than management?

Financial secrets are mainly a protection against stock exchange speculation in the event of cash shortage. But they may include information that ought not to be secret, even from an accounting point of view, like the purchase of shares by another company that seeks to conceal its identity.

Item 4(c) above is probably the most important, concealing the position in different plants or companies when the details of costs, sales and profits for each of the separate parts of a business are all wrapped up together in the overall figures of the parent company or group accounts.

The famous economist J. M. Keynes is reported to have said to the AUDITOR of a company at a meeting of its board of directors: 'We all know, Mr X, that auditors consider that the object of accounts is to conceal the truth, but surely not even you can believe that the object is to conceal the truth from the directors.'

It is not; but it may be to conceal the truth from the workers and the Government, and particularly from the tax inspector. The offensive launched by private industry against Anthony Benn as Secretary of State for Industry early in 1975 appeared to be motivated more by fear of his desire to consult trade unions and workers about information disclosed to the Department of Industry than about this information reaching the eyes and ears of other industrialists. Competition has never been quite what it is made out to be. You know that from experience of the way employers join up in price-fixing trade associations and in their united resistance to wage demands.

In 1972 when the Commission on Industrial Relations was preparing a report on disclosure of information, the TUC drew up a list of points of information which it thought should be provided. The CIR in its report compared this with the information made available by law under the Companies Acts (Appendix 7 to Report No. 31). Here are the items that the TUC wants and that are not available under the Companies Acts. You should be able to get most of them now under the Employment Protection Act.

The Information Gap

Apart from certain details about shareholdings, NOMINEE holdings, etc., the main gaps are as follows:

There is no breakdown of the overall number of employees by jobs and grades, turnover, absenteeism, sickness and accident rates;
Wages and salaries are not broken down into the make-up of pay, overtime and bonuses, by jobs and grades;
Output is not shown per man with unit costs of labour, costs of materials and administration and value added to direct and indirect labour costs;
Sales figures are not published for sales outside the group or company nor for internal purchases and sales and the pricing policy, nor for transfers between plants and AFFILIATES at home and overseas;
Plans and prospects are not made public, especially for MERGERS and new finance, for investment and trading at home and overseas, for RESEARCH AND DEVELOPMENT, for stockpiling; for manpower changes, recruitment, promotion, redeployment, redundancy.

All these are in the TUC's list, but they are not covered by the Companies Acts. The Stock Exchange Federation has also recommended that the historical record of companies should be available over a ten-year run, not just for each year. Moreover, the TUC has not specified here, as it has elsewhere, the need for all these figures to be made available for *individual plants and locations*, together with a similar geographical breakdown of profits, taking into account Government grants, etc. Only in this way can workers, and the Government too, really know what any company is doing with the value that is being added at each stage of production and distribution.

Now check how many of the items in the TUC list should be available according to the ACAS Code of Practice under the Employment Protection Act 1975.

Then decide how much of this information is relevant for your particular purposes in negotiation or consultation and check on:

The date of the information and comparability with earlier data;
The breakdown of figures by plant, division or company;
The need to pool your information with others in your organization and at different levels of your union.

4. Using What You Know

In the last two chapters we have made two studies. One was of possible pieces of knowledge which you may already have about the organization you work for, or which you could obtain fairly easily. The other was of the things which management will probably be keeping secret. You may have noticed that many items coincide. In other words, you already know something about just those secrets that management wants to keep to itself. When we talked earlier, however, about the things you already know, we made the point that they were bitty and that they needed to be put into a wider framework consisting of the type of organization for which you work and the way in which its accounts (particularly company accounts) are drawn up. We shall make a start on doing this now.

The Organization You Work For

We will assume that you are not an employer of labour or self-employed, but that you are, like about 90 per cent of the working people of Britain, an employee. Then you might work for any of the following types of organization:

1. In the state sector:
   A central Government department;
   A county, district or other local authority;
   The Health Service or other state institution;
   A public CORPORATION (like London Transport, the BBC or a nationalized industry).
   About 20 per cent of all employees work for one of these.
2. In the private sector:
   A PARTNERSHIP;
   A PRIVATE COMPANY;
   A PUBLIC COMPANY;
   A non-profit-making private organization (including non-commercial companies).

About 80 per cent of all employees work for one of these. The state sector has been growing in recent years in the numbers employed and in income, and large companies have been growing in size and importance as a result of mergers and takeovers. Nonetheless, it is surprising how many self-employed and small businesses remain. Here is a table to show two different ways of measuring the importance of the various parts of the private sector, including individual traders, who may or may not employ labour.

Table 5: Sole Traders, Partnerships and Companies, UK 1970

	Number	*Total income (£m)*
Private sector		
Individual or sole traders	1 500 000	1 500
Partnerships	250 000	500
Private companies	50 000	1 000
Other unquoted companies	120 000	1 000
Non-commercial companies	20 000	—
Subsidiaries (mainly owned by public companies)	55 000	—
Quoted 'public' companies	5 000	7500
of which 'top industrial 1000'	1 000	5 000
'top industrial 250'	250	4 000
'top industrial 50'	50	2 500
Total companies	250 000	9 500
Grand total	2 000 000	11 500
Public sector		
State corporations and other public undertakings (excluding local government)	10	1600

NOTE: Central Government departments and services and local authorities are not included in this table, because they are not easy to enumerate and they mainly do not generate their own income but rather collect funds by taxation for their expenditures. COOPERATIVES are also excluded, because they really are very small and quite few, apart from the Cooperative Wholesale Society and the Cooperative Retail Societies.

We shall be looking mainly at the accounts of state corporations and so-called 'public' companies in this book. With minor variations the accounts of the Coops and of 'private' companies follow the same accounting practices as those of the 'public' companies. The accounts of the central Government and of local authorities are quite different. They are also of great interest and we shall have a brief word about them at the end of the book. Definitions of these different forms of organization appear in the Glossary (*see* pp. 129–40).

It is not difficult to see from Table 5 that in terms of income the 'top companies' and the state corporations quite dwarf the hundreds of thousands of smaller businesses; most of these are in fact probably sub-contractors or suppliers to the 'Big Boys', and very much dependent on them not only for orders but for the prices they can charge and the profits they can make. The leading company or companies in each line of production can fix prices at a level which suits them, subject to government controls; and the rest must follow as best they can. Despite this, the number of companies grows every year. This is partly because new companies are being registered all the time, while companies that have ceased operations are not necessarily taken off the register. The main reason for the increase is that the formation of a company with one or two participants, or at most the members of a family, can be a very advantageous way for rich people or the professional 'lump' to reduce their tax.

What is a Company?

A company is called a company because it is a company of shareholders in a jointly held STOCK OF CAPITAL. But it is also a distinct legal entity, or personality as it is called in English law. This means that subject to the articles of association, by which the original shareholders set it up, it can do things on its own account. It can own property and employ labour; it can run up debts or pollute the atmosphere or endanger the safety of its workers; and for these the company is responsible, *not* the individuals who put up the capital, although managers now have certain responsibilities under the Health and Safety Act. If the directors themselves ever want to give the money away, and a shareholder challenges them because such a use of funds was not provided for in the articles, then the money cannot be given away. If you suffer an accident at work, or you are owed money by the company, you have to sue the company; it is no good going after any of the individual owners or shareholders.

Most companies and some partnerships have the word 'limited' after their name. This makes it clear to all who subscribe to the capital that the company's LIABILITY for debts is limited to the amount of capital subscribed. The company is liable to that extent, and no individual shareholder or manager can be sued for debts beyond that amount. If the company goes bankrupt a shareholder may lose all he subscribed but not more than that, even if the company had debts in excess of its capital. The purpose of this arrangement, which goes back to a Companies Act of 1856, was to encourage the supply of capital for undertakings in amounts that were beyond the means of any individual or partners. This Act and others provided the basis for the full development of modern large-scale CAPITALISM, by confirming the power of owners of capital to participate in the profits derived from the employment of labour in commercial enterprises.

For the capitalists the result was that the risk of loss was minimized and professional management could more easily be brought in and given the stewardship of the several capitals associated together in the company. You will notice that the chairman and secretary of a company are always chairman and secretary of the board of directors. The board is responsible in law for the shareholder's money. This is an important point to notice because the law would have to be changed if the directors had also to be responsible to the workers. Nowadays most directors are managers and are not themselves big shareholders, although among the directors there may be large shareholders, members of the family that founded the firm and representatives of institutions like insurance companies and unit trusts. These institutional shareholdings are increasingly important, but you don't need to believe the myth that most shares are held by poor widows and orphans. They are mostly very rich men and women. Many companies are now owned by holding companies or conglomerates, that only really manage the finance of their subsidiaries.

A LEGAL PERSONALITY

We have taken a strictly legal definition of a company in order to emphasize that its objective must be first and last to make money for the company of shareholders. If any one company does not make money, its shareholders will look for other companies and other ways of making money. Some may be prepared to wait for their money to accumulate over many years; others will be looking for a quick return. Managements will have to adjust their policies to meet the preference of those whose capital they are managing, and above all to stay in business in competition with other companies. This means that they must meet the expected going rate of profit, and they must replace old equipment, invest in new equipment *and* make regular payments to those who put up the money. In order to do this with the most modern plant and machinery, companies get larger and larger, so that they can call on the money of more and more shareholders and other sources of funds, and they widen their range of products and the markets they sell in, so as to spread their risks. A monopoly position, as the sole suppliers of a particular product in a particular market, should ensure high profits because prices can be pushed well up above unit costs. But it is the giant companies' security, given by the diversity of their products, and their power to control the sources of supplies and attract funds, that has established them in the dominant position we noticed in the table above (p. 33). This is where the institutional shareholders come in, the insurance companies, superannuation funds and unit trusts, since their aim is not a high and risky profit, but a guaranteed income that beats the rate of inflation.

A SOCIAL ORGANIZATION

While the company properly is the company of shareholders, the organization of the company is a social organization. You won't find much about this in the Report and Accounts; but this is what it is; it brings together hundreds, and often today thousands, of workers of many kinds with many different skills and aptitudes to produce the goods or services which the company supplies. You are probably not an isolated individual in your company. Management, non-manual workers and manual workers alike all have group interests. You may work, for instance, in a large or small group, in a workshop or a department according to the division of labour we looked at earlier. You may join a union to protect your interests against the power of the employer. The relationship of workers to their employers has always had two aspects: cooperation and conflict. Workers need to work together with management to produce the goods and services from which their incomes all derive; they need also to challenge the distribution of the value which they add by their productive work but which they do not control. Increasingly workers through their trade unions are demanding something else, a say both in how their work is organized and what it is organized for. That is, they are challenging the distribution of power in their company as well as the distribution of value. The aim of this book is to help you to have your say.

The Framework of Company Accounts

We have already seen that the information that management supplies to the company of shareholders is not designed to reveal the way the company works as a social organization nor the benefits and hazards that the company's workers sustain from their efforts. The sole aim of the accounts is to show how the shareholders' money has been applied to making more money, over the past period and in the present and foreseeable future. This aim establishes the form that the accounts take. The accounts consist of:

1. A balance sheet of assets and liabilities; for the shareholder this means the condition of his capital;
2. A profit and loss account; for the shareholder this means what money did the company make;
3. A statement of the cash flow or the source and disposition of funds or income (that is the profit before tax and provision for depreciation); for the shareholder this means what the company is doing with the money it made.

Examples of each of these appear on pp. 42–4 below.

THE BALANCE SHEET

Our basic business accounting model in Chapter 1 was in effect a balance sheet at a particular point in time. Shareholders want to know what has happened to the value of their capital over a period of time. So it is the opening and closing values in any period that they want to know about, and these values they will expect to see represented in two ways:

1. As the capital they have supplied, plus any sums accumulated in the company from profits before the period begins. These last will be called RETAINED PROFITS. In addition the capital may have increased in value because of rising prices. Such increases will be called capital reserves;
2. As the assets of actual buildings, plant, machinery and other investments, to which their capital and any additions to it have been put.

In many company accounts, by English tradition, capital is set out on the left-hand side and assets on the right. But nowadays it is increasingly common to set out the assets first and follow them with the capital.

However, the accounts are always complicated by one important fact. They are the accounts of the company and, therefore, from the point of view of the company, the capital, capital reserves and any retained profit are all liabilities, that is, they are owed by the company to the shareholders. In addition, there will be other liabilities, that is, debts owed to other people besides the shareholders: to banks for overdrafts, to traders for credit, and so on. On the assets side there will, likewise, be cash, loans and debts owed *to* the company as well as the value of buildings, plant, equipment, etc. If you take away from all these assets just those liabilities owed by the company to outsiders, what you have left is what is called the net worth of the company, the capital, reserves and the retained profit. These may be called the shareholders' funds.

THE PROFIT AND LOSS ACCOUNT

The shareholders want to know what money the company made. This appeared in the middle of our Basic Business Accounting Model in Chapter 1 from the 'Receipts' less 'Expenditure' over the period. In England, the debits are set out on the left-hand side and the credits on the right, but modern practice puts the credits first and then the debits. On the credit side there will be receipts from sales and other income, and on the debit side will appear the costs of goods sold and other payments. These other expenditures will have to include:

Provision for depreciation or wear and tear;
Interest on money borrowed (not from shareholders);
Pension fund contributions;
Hire of plant, etc.;
Fees to auditors;
Tax due.

There may be what are called 'Extraordinary Items' because they cannot be expected to appear as profits or losses again. Some accounts will show GROSS PROFIT *before* all these other payments; and TRADING PROFIT or NET PROFIT *after* all these payments. Sometimes they will distinguish PRE-TAX PROFIT and POST-TAX PROFIT, meaning net of all the other deductions, but before and after tax is paid. Of course, there may be a loss and not a profit at all at any of these stages.

THE SOURCE AND DISPOSITION OF FUNDS OR CASH FLOW

What is happening to the money the company made? The cash flow statement shows the way in which the pre-tax profit plus the depreciation provision and any new borrowings have been used during the period and are to be used in, for example:

Paying dividends to shareholders;
Paying taxes due (less grants received);
Increasing or decreasing the value of stocks;
Increasing or decreasing credits or debts;
Increasing or decreasing cash and loans to others;
Increasing or decreasing assets.

Snakes and Ladders

The only way to work through this maze of balance sheets, profit and loss accounts and source and disposition statements is to take an imaginary situation. Your Uncle John offers you a loan of £70000 to go into business producing a motorcar trimming you have invented and patented; he requires you to pay him back in twenty years' time plus 5 per cent a year fixed dividend. Given the rate of inflation it is a very decent offer.

The next two pages of this book are in the form of a flow diagram that looks rather like a Snakes and Ladders game.

Snakes and Ladders Company   Accounting for actions

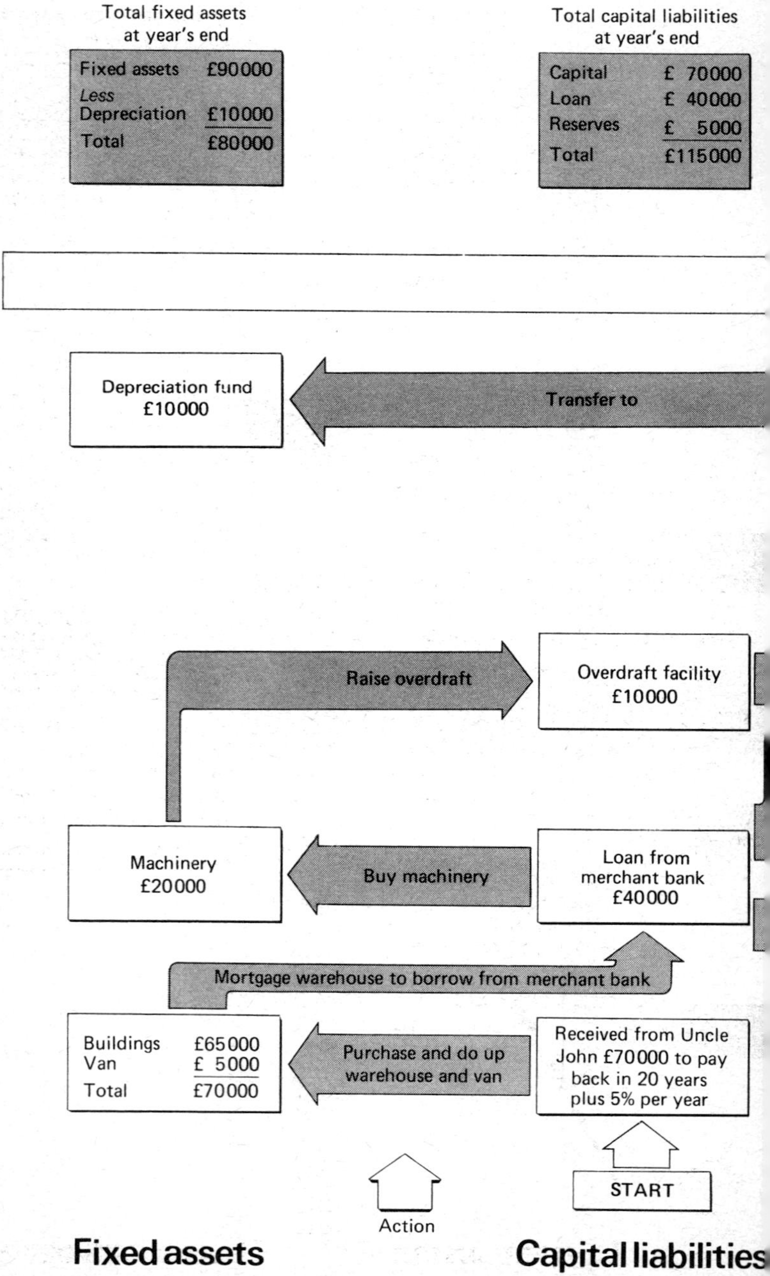

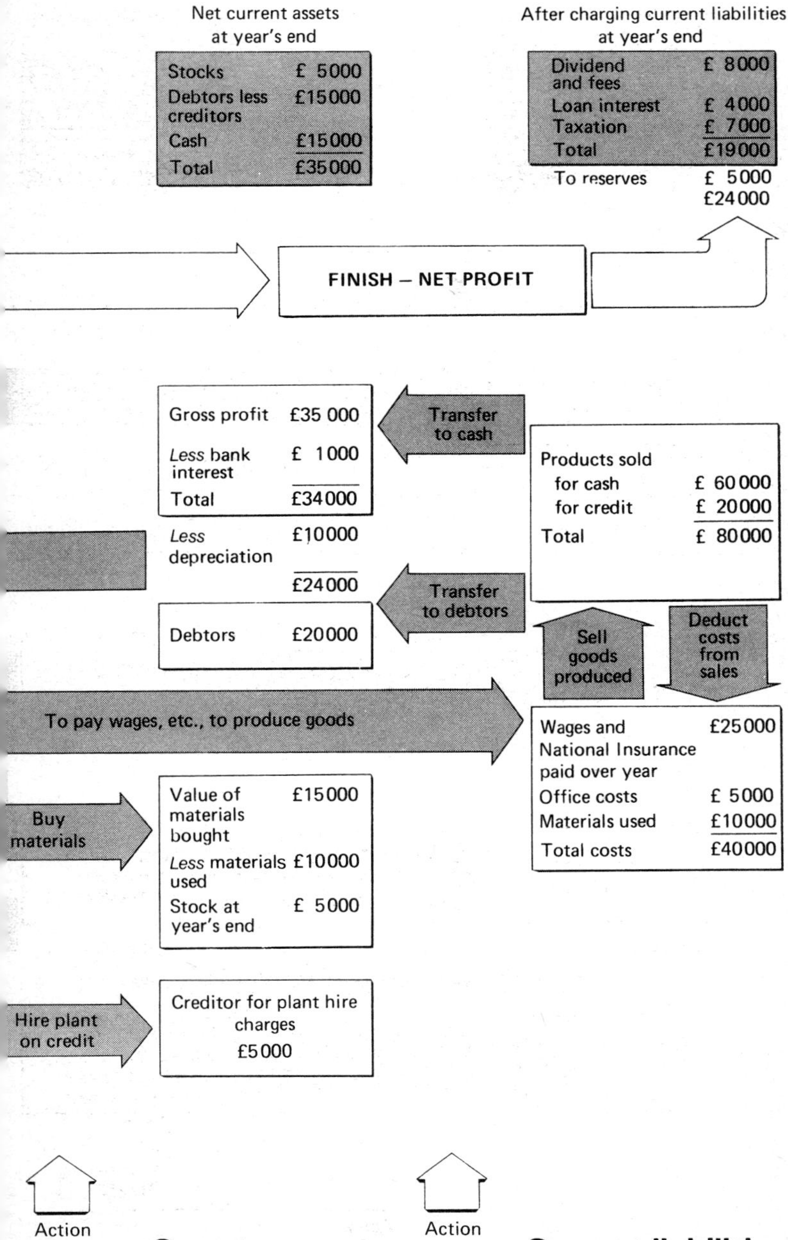

Current assets

Current liabilities

What you do to follow the diagram is to go up the arrows when you get money and sideways when you have to pay out on current or capital account. After the diagram there are printed the three basic statements and a fourth, the fixed assets depreciation account.

Follow the diagram through and you should become able to make sense of the way the different statements are related. Notice that the board is divided up into sections, to help you identify the nature of the transaction that is taking place. These sections are called Fixed Assets, Capital Liabilities, Current Assets, Current Liabilities. If you can find your way through this, no company accounts should present any problems.

Table 6: Snakes and Ladders Company, End Year Balance Sheet (£)

Liabilities	Original capital		70000	(70000)*
	Loan capital		40000	
	Reserves		5000	
			115000	(70000)
Assets	Fixed assets		90000	
	Less depreciation		10000	
			80000	
	Net current assets			
	Stock		5000	
	Debtors *less* creditors		15000	
	Cash		15000	(70000)
After charging	Tax	7000		
	Fees	4500		
	Dividend	3500		
	Loan interest	4000		
			35000	
			115000	

*Figures in brackets are for the beginning of the year.

NOTES ON THE ACCOUNTS

1. It is assumed that cash from sales began to come in soon after starting payments for wages, and that any gaps were covered by the overdraft. You were lucky to get the plant hire on credit; but it will have to be paid for the next year out of the surplus due from debts. This will be discussed under the heading of 'Cash Flow' in Chapter 7.

2. Some accountants would say that you have very heavy fixed charges on the business, what they call a high capital 'GEARING'. Even if you reckon Uncle John's £70000 as money he is risking, he is asking for a 5 per cent fixed dividend and repayment in twenty years; and you have another £50000 owing at fixed interest rates to the merchant bank and with the overdraft.

Table 7: Snakes and Ladders Company, Profit and Loss Account for the Year (£)

Sales			80000
Costs	Wages	25000	
	Office	5000	
	Materials used	10000	
	Overdraft interest	1000	
	Hire charges	5000	
	Depreciation	10000	
			56000
Trading profit			24000
Less tax			7000
After tax profit			17000
To dividend		3500	
	Loan interest	4000	
	Fees to self	4000	
	Fees to auditor	500	
			12000
To reserve			5000
	Retained profit	1500	
	Sinking fund	3500	

Table 8: Snakes and Ladders Company, Source and Disposition Statement over Year (£)

Source of funds		
Original capital	70000	
Loan	40000	
Profit before tax	24000	
Add back depreciation	10000	
		144000
Disposition of funds		
Fixed assets	90000	
Taxation	7000	
Proprietor's and auditor's charges	8000	
Loan interest	4000	
Changes in working capital		
Stocks	5000	
Debtors *less* creditors	15000	
Cash	15000	
		144000

Table 9: Fixed Asset Depreciation Fund (£)

	Asset cost	*Depreciation provision*
Buildings	65000	4500
Van	5000	1750
Machinery	20000	3750
	90000	10000

Remember that in a large organization there may be different accounts at different levels:
Operating unit or profit centre.
Company or division.
Combine or national board.
International holding company.

Part II: What You Need to Know About

5. Profit and Value Added for Wage Negotiation

What Makes Up Profit?

In the imaginary business which we have just been looking at (*see* p. 43), the final profit appears at the end of the year, after sales of £80000, as a reserve of £5000 retained in the company for future use and for paying back Uncle John. It is the excess of assets over liabilities in the balance sheet. But there was a much larger figure of trading profit before tax of £24000, which was eaten up in the following ways:

Table 10: Trading Profit, Snakes and Ladders Company (£)

Trading profit		24000
To taxation	7000	
To interest	4000	
To fees – self	4000	
– auditor	500	
To dividend	3500	19000
To reserve		5000

Furthermore, the costs of the first year's working of the business included another £1000 paid on the bank overdraft, which could be included in profit; and there was that big figure of £10000 provided for depreciation. The fact that it was provided for does not mean, of course, that it was spent on making replacements. Some day it probably will have to be spent, but not necessarily all in one year. The figure is set at what the tax inspector will allow, so that it can be thought of in part as a tax-free addition to profits. What is more, the present tax system in Britain gives companies tax allowances or investment grants, and also regional grants for investment in plant and machinery. As a result quite a

large part of the figure for depreciation may be real profit. In our story the proprietor's fees were shown coming out of the profits, but they could quite legitimately have been counted as costs. Directors' fees have to be revealed in company reports under company law, because they would otherwise be lost in the general accounts. There might also be other items to count in as profits, like management pension schemes and rent paid for office and other premises. Marxist economists always talk about *surplus* and not just about profits. This includes all the value added by workers in a company, less the wages and salaries that they receive.

The first point to make, then, is that profits can be quite legitimately concealed in various ways. The second point is that profits are often shown as a percentage of sales. But the value of sales includes all the bought-in supplies, that is, stocks of raw materials used, power supplies, hire charges, bank charges, and so on. If we leave these out, we can concentrate on the value added, that is the value added by work inside the business itself. We then have a very different picture. Value added in our imaginary Snakes and Ladders example is £65000, made up of:

Wages	£25000
Office	£5000
Depreciation	£10000
Interest, Fees and Profit	£18000
Tax	£7000

A regular trick company chairmen play in their reports is to show profits as a few pence in the pound. Here is an example from the accounts of the Arthur Lee Group, Sheffield wire-makers, giving figures for 1973–4.

Table 11: Sales Revenue Breakdown by percentage, Arthur Lee Group, 1973–4

Raw material	63·5	72·5 (Raw material + Manufacturing expenses)
Manufacturing expenses	9	
Wages, etc.	15·5	
Overheads	2·5	
Depreciation	2	
Taxes	5	
Dividends	1	
Retained profits	1·5	
Total sales	100	

It's like a vanishing trick. The profit appears to be only 2½p in the £. But if we look a bit closer we may see how the trick is worked. The profit is shown as a percentage of sales and not of value added.

Bought-in materials and plant hire were a fairly small part of total costs in our example. But in the case of the Arthur Lee Group in 1973–4 they were large – 72½ per cent of sales. If we deduct for raw materials and manufacturing expenses, the make-up of value added works out as follows (and we can compare the latest year with the previous year):

Table 12: Value Added Make-up by Percentage: Arthur Lee Group, 1972–3 – 1973–4

	1973–4	*1972–3*
Wages, etc.	56	56·5
Overheads	9·5	10
Depreciation	7·5	8
Taxes	18·5	13
Dividends	3·5	5·5
Retained profit	5	7
	100	100

In other words, judging from the top line, the workers got a bit more than half of the value they added by their work. Management will tell you that it's not you but the machines that create the extra value. You could of course let them see what happened if you left the machines to themselves, or you could start making some comparisons of value added per worker. This depends primarily upon the machines that the worker has to work with.

Value Added

THE AGE AND CAPACITY OF THE MACHINES

Value added per worker in modern industrial plants in Japan is about double what it is in Britain. Investment per worker has been very much higher over the years there than here, as indicated by the huge figure for fixed assets per worker.

Table 13: Value Added Per Worker in Selected Companies, 1974

	Plessey	*GEC*	*Philips*	*Hitachi*	*Sony*
Sales (£m)	4·5	6·8	11·2	20·1	40·6
Less bought-in supplies (£m)	1·7	3·6	5·2	13·7	30·2
Equals value added (£m)	2·8	3·2	6·0	6·4	10·4
Divided by workers (nos)	58000	206000	412000	82000	11000
Equals value added per worker (£)	2777	3268	5957	6431	10402
Paid in wages,[1] etc. (£)	2121	2136	4457	3807	3938
taxes (£)	204	476	384	624	2608
profit,[2] etc. (£)	452	656	1116	2000	4966
Net fixed assets[3] per worker (£)	15000	5400	10100	37500	36300

NOTES:

1. Wages include salaries, welfare and pensions.
2. Profit includes rent, financial costs (interest) and depreciation.
3. Net fixed assets = buildings, plant and machinery at depreciated value.

SOURCE: Dr Frank Jones, *The Times*, 10 February 1976.

Information at Work: Erratum

Table 13 on page 48 should be replaced by the following:

Table 13: Value Added Per Worker in Selected Companies, 1974

	Plessey	*GEC*	*Philips*	*Hitachi*	*Sony*
Sales (£m)	260	1400	4620	1650	446
Less bought-in supplies (£m)	98	740	2140	1120	332
Equals value added (£m)	162	660	2480	530	114
Divided by workers (nos.)	58000	206000	412000	82000	11000
Equals value added per worker (£)	2777	3268	5957	6431	10402
Paid in wages,[1] etc. (£)	2121	2136	4457	3807	3938
taxes (£)	204	476	384	624	2608
profit,[2] etc. (£)	452	656	1116	2000	3856
Net fixed assets[3] per worker (£)	15000	5400	10100	37500	36300

NOTES:

1. Wages include salaries, welfare and pensions.
2. Profit includes rent, financial costs (interest) and depreciation.
3. Net fixed assets = buildings, plant and machinery at depreciated value.

SOURCE: Dr Frank Jones, *The Times*, 10 February 1976.

PERFORMANCE INDICATORS FOR WORKERS: THE SHARE OF DIRECT AND INDIRECT LABOUR IN VALUE ADDED

We have just seen how important the assets are per worker in determining value added. But it may be important for you also to distinguish labour that is directly involved in production and that which is only indirectly involved. In some factories and offices it seems that it's all chiefs and no Indians. You may be able to distinguish the payrolls of direct production workers, of non-production workers in the works and of office workers. You should certainly be able to find:

1. Payroll cost (wages, direct and indirect, plus other wage costs like National Insurance) and you can work that out per £1 of value added. Then if you could find:
2. Direct payroll cost, you could work out added value per £1 of direct pay. Then if you could also find:
3. Man-hours of direct labour, you could work out added value (in £) per man-hour (direct labour). And if you could get:
4. Figures for all these for different periods, then you could study the changes from year to year.

All these relations that you could find out are called performance ratios. They are very useful for management to control what they can pay in wages; and you should therefore have access to the same information.

Not all companies provide figures for bought-in costs which would enable you to discover the value added, and those that do generally supply the information only for the whole company or group of companies, when what you will be interested in is the value added in your own works or plant. But it is worth pressing the managers for these figures. They should know them if they are any good at their jobs, and you ought to know them if you are to bargain realistically. Even the overall company figures can reveal something of what is going on.

PERFORMANCE INDICATORS FOR CAPITALISTS: THE RETURN TO CAPITAL

Owners of capital want to know how their capital is being used and how much they are getting out of investment, especially out of new investment in machines and plant. You ought to know this too; and these figures will be much more easily available, because capitalists must know them in order to decide where to put their money. It will not be hard to find the following performance ratios:

Changes in sales over the years;
Changes in capital employed over the years;
Changes in profits over the years.

From these you can work out:

Profit as a percentage of sales;
Profit as a percentage of capital employed.

If the company reveals a figure for value added, you can find:

Changes in value added over the years;
Value added as percentage of sales;
Profit as a percentage of value added;
Value added in relation to capital employed.

One of the most useful ratios for you to check up on is the *increase* in value added in relation to the *increase* in capital employed, for that will be the result of introducing new machinery, for which management will be claiming the credit in any increase in output. The key question for you will be how much of the extra value added went to the workers and how much to the owners of the capital.

Let's look at the Arthur Lee Group again. This is a big table but you should work through it with the notes, step by step.

[Notes continued on page 52]

Table 14: Arthur Lee Group Operating Results, Years Ending September 1973 and September 1974

	1973 £m	*1974* £m	*Increase 1973–4* £m	*as %*	*Notes see below*
Sales	27·5	43·0	15·5	*+56*	2 (a)
Stocks at beginning of year	5·9	7·1	1·2	*+20*	
Purchased materials	16·9	27·2	10·3	*+61*	
Less					
Stocks at end of year	−7·1	−10·9	3·8	*+53*	
Therefore					
Materials used in goods sold	15·7	23·4	7·7	*+49*	
Other manufacturing costs	2·5	3·9	1·4	*+56*	
All costs of goods sold	18·2	27·3	9·1	*+50*	
Therefore					
Value added (i.e. sales less all costs)	9·3	15·7	6·4	*+69*	1 (c)
as % of sales	*33·8*	*36·5*	—	—	2 (b)
Overheads	0·8	1·1	0·3	*+38*	3 (b)
Depreciation	0·7	0·9	0·2	*+29*	3 (c)
Payroll cost	4·6	6·6	2·0	*+43*	
as % of value added	*49·5*	*42·0*	—	—	3 (a)
Value added per £1 of payroll cost	*2·0*	*2·38*	—	—	4 (a)
per employee in £s					
3000 (in 1973)	3100				
2600 (in 1974)		6038	—	*+69·5*	
Payroll cost per employee in £s	1533	2538	—	*+65·5*	4 (b)
Capital employed					
at beginning of year	12·45	13·86	1·41	*+11*	
at end of year	13·86	18·55	4·69	*+34*	1 (a)
of which stocks	7·1	10·9	3·8	*+53*	
excluding stocks	6·8	7·6	0·8	*+12*	1 (b)
Profit (after depreciation and before tax)	2·1	3·6	1·5	*+71*	3 (d)
as % of capital employed (end year)	*15·1*	*19·4*	—	—	5
Value added as % of capital employed (end year)	*67·0*	*85·0*	—	—	1 (d)

[Notes continued from page 50]

Notes to the Table. Follow through the numbered notes by the side of the table, starting in the middle with the entry 'Capital employed':

1 (a) With a 34 per cent increase in capital employed;
(b) Which is only in fact a 12 per cent increase if stocks are excluded;
(c) Value added was increased by 69 per cent, so that
(d) It rose from 67 per cent to 85 per cent of capital employed (including stocks).

So it was how the machines were employed that mattered, not just the extra capital equipment.

2 (a) Value added rose faster than sales (69 per cent and 56 per cent) so that
(b) Value added as a percentage of sales rose slightly from 33·8 per cent to 36·5 per cent.

The key question that the trade unionist will want to ask is what happened to the *extra* value added over these two years, that is who got the benefit from it.

3 (a) Wages, or at least total payroll costs, as a percentage of value added, fell from 49·5 per cent to 42·0 per cent because, although
(b) Overhead costs and
(c) Depreciation rose less than value added as a whole,
(d) What was left for profit rose more, by 71 per cent in fact.

This share of wages in value added is shown clearly when

4 (a) Value added is calculated per £1 of wages paid and is shown as rising from £2·0 to £2·38, even though
(b) Wages per employee were rising fast.

It does seem then that in this company over these two years, despite sharply rising wages, the workers' share as a whole was slipping while the share of profit was rising. It was only in small part the cut-back in employees from 3000 to 2600 that gave them the big boost per head in 4(b). We may note one final element:

5 Profit as a percentage of capital employed rose from 15·1 per cent to 19·4 per cent.

Management will have a ready answer if you point that out. The firm's report to their employees said that these were windfall profits due to the APPRECIATION of stock values. This is a very complex question which we cannot discuss in this book. You should just notice what we did to get the value added figure. We had to find the cost of materials *used up* during the year by adding materials purchased during the year to the stocks at the beginning of the year and then deducting stocks left over at the year's end. If the value of stocks appreciated in price over the year because of inflation, then you can see that there is a problem of deciding whether this was a real increase in capital values or not. It will make a lot of difference whether the company's stocks were mainly of raw materials which would have to be replaced at a higher price or of finished products which could be *sold* at a higher price.

WORKING OUT VALUE ADDED FOR YOUR OWN COMPANY

You should now be able to work out some value added figures for your own company. Either the Annual Report and Accounts or the Report to Employees should give you the figures for sales, for stocks at the beginning and the end of year, for raw material purchases, for other manufacturing costs. This will give you the value added. Then you can find the ratio of value added to sales and to capital employed. Find the value added in the previous year and check whether you are winning or losing by looking at the share of value added in each year going to payroll, overheads (administrative expenses), depreciation provision and profit.

Once more, remember that you will need to obtain information for the unit, plant or division that is relevant for your purpose and that you can pool your information with what is available at other levels of your organization. Then you can relate all this to overall company figures.

6. Productivity Bargaining for Control over Manning

If you've had anything to do with productivity bargaining you will know that it has often involved reductions in manning – 'selling your mates down the road', to be honest about it – in order to justify wage increases under the prices and incomes policies operating since the early 1970s. In the last chapter we related value added to the number of employees at Arthur Lee's and noticed that this rose from £2700 per employee in 1972–3 to over £4500 in 1973–4. In part this increase resulted from a cut in the labour force from 3000 to 2600. So Arthur Lee's got shot of 400 men between the *years* ending September 1973 and 1974, but even with the same number, value added would have risen from £2700 to £3967, that is by 47 per cent, when prices in general rose by less than 20 per cent. We do not have figures for the hours worked or for the amount of overtime done. When relating value added to the number of workers in order to get the labour productivity figures, you will naturally think not only of the work but of the workers' hours and conditions. We also have to remember that in bad years the work produced cannot be sold. Productivity may thus be the result of many different changes, dividing value or volume of output by labour (that is, numbers of workers) and hours worked. For instance:

Increased labour productivity may result from:

$$\frac{\text{same output}}{\text{less labour, same hours}} \text{ or } \frac{\text{same output}}{\text{same labour, fewer hours}}$$

$$\text{or } \frac{\text{more output}}{\text{same labour, same hours}} \text{ or } \frac{\text{same output volume (higher prices)}}{\text{same labour, same hours}}$$

$$\text{or } \frac{\text{less output}}{\text{even less labour, fewer hours}}$$

Decreased productivity may result from:

$$\frac{\text{same output}}{\text{more labour, more hours}}$$

$$\text{or } \frac{\text{same output volume (lower prices)}}{\text{same labour, same hours}}$$

$$\text{or } \frac{\text{less output sold}}{\text{same labour, same hours}}$$

The productivity formula is:

$$\frac{\text{output value or volume}}{\text{number of workers} \times \text{hours worked}}$$

The line means 'divided by'. If the figure above the line grows more or falls less than the combined figure under the line, then productivity increases. If it grows less or falls more, productivity decreases.

Productivity and Earnings

When dealing with productivity you have to make comparisons with other firms over periods of time. There are many published INDICES for the changes in output over time and for employment changes in the economy as a whole and in different industries, from which it is possible to compare movements of employment and values of output and the VOLUMES of output, that is after deducting for price changes. You will want to know how the movements in your earnings in money and in real terms have been keeping up with them. The problem will be getting to know the figures for your own company as well as for your industry. The *New Earnings Survey* of the Department of Employment can be used to get figures for wages in large companies like ICI, so that comparisons between movements in productivity and movements in earnings can be made. We can use these, as the Ruskin College Trade Union Research Unit has done, to discover how productivity has been rising in ICI in relation to the rest of the chemical industry and what chemical workers have been getting out of increased productivity. Here are some figures for productivity changes in the UK chemical industry as a whole and in ICI over a five-year period:

Table 15: Productivity[1] Indices for UK Chemical Industry and ICI, 1970–4

	1970	*1971*	*1972*	*1973*	*1974*
Chemical industry					
Output volume	100	102·2	108·1	121·6	130·0
Employment	100	97·4	95·0	89·3	92·3
Productivity (i.e. output per employee)	100	105·2	114·0	136·0	141·0
Real earnings (wages, salaries only per all employees)[3]	100	102·5	106·5	107·9	112·0
ICI[2]					
Output sales total	100	104·0	115·7	148·1	200·8
prices (home)	100	108·2	113·7	118·9	151·6
hence volume	100	96·0	102·0	125·0	133·0
Employment	100	98·0	101·0	101·0	102·0
Productivity (i.e. output per employee)	100	98·0	101·0	123·5	130·5
Real earnings[3] (per UK employees) A.[4]	100	103·0	105·0	106·0	109·0
B.	100	105·0	112·0	115·0	121·0

NOTES:

1. Productivity is found by dividing employment index into volume × 100. Source: Taken from Department of Employment *Gazette* and from *Trade and Industry*. Earnings from the *New Earnings Survey*, calculated by the Ruskin College Trade Union Research Unit.
2. ICI prices are assumed from the *Trade and Industry* Wholesale Price Chemicals and Allied Index of Output (home sales).
3. Real earnings are the result of adjusting for retail price increases.
4. ICI UK earnings: A. includes wages and salaries only; B. comprises all employee remuneration including pensions and profit sharing.

It appears from these figures (which do not tell us anything about hours worked but only about the number of workers):

1. That ICI's productivity (based on 1970 = 100) at 130·5 in 1974 was falling behind the general rise for the chemical industry as a whole since this was at 141 in 1974;

2. That employee earnings in chemicals were falling well behind the increases in productivity in this period and that ICI employees were only doing better than the rest when pension fund and profit-sharing payments were taken into account.

In negotiating workers' wages, trade unionists want to know the value of the output contributed by particular groups of workers. The *New Earnings Survey* provides figures for the earnings of workers in different groups of occupations, but there is no information generally available for individual companies, let alone for separate departments. The shop stewards at ICI asked specially to be provided with this information. You should be able to do the same.

Real Value Added per Employee

What matters, as we have seen, is the value added, not the sales value. The ICI stewards had been able to work out from the company's Annual Reports how value added per worker had moved over the years. These figures, of course, were for the whole of ICI's worldwide operations. The results came out as follows:

Table 16: ICI Value Added and Earnings per Employee, 1973–6

Year	*Sales £m*	*Purchases £m*	*Value added £m*	*Employees '000s*	*Value added per employee £*	*UK earnings per UK employee*	
						£	*as %**
1973	2166	1187	979	199	4920	2371	48
1974	2955	1716	1239	201	6164	2833	46
1975	3099	1831	1268	195	6503	3558	55
1976	4135	2458	1677	192	8734	4216	48

*The last column shows earnings as % of value added per employee.

The share of employees' earnings in value added has fluctuated considerably over these four years. It is true that the figures are not strictly comparable because the value added figure is for all employees and the earnings figure is for UK employees only. But the rising share of earnings has to be explained. What happens is this: when sales are stagnant, productivity (whether measured as sales per employee or as value added per employee) is likely to fall; earnings per employee may still be maintained by trade union action. In a period of rising prices what is really happening is concealed. If we deflate for price increases, we can see from the figures in Table 16 what happened in real terms. We will convert the figures for 1974, 1975 and 1976 into 1973 prices by dividing by the retail price index, which is based on 1973=100. This rose to 116 in 1974, 144 in 1975 and 167 in 1976.

Table 17: ICI Value Added and Earnings per Employee, 1973–6, at 1973 Prices

Year	*Sales £m*	*Purchases £m*	*Value added £m*	*Employees '000s*	*Value added per employee £*	*UK earnings per UK employee*	
						£	*as %*
1973	2166	1187	979	199	4920	2371	48
1974	2547	1479	1068	201	5314	2442	46
1975	2152	1271	881	195	4515	2471	55
1976	2476	1471	1005	192	5234	2525	48

Sales declined in volume in 1975 below the 1973 level, but bought-in supplies were higher than in 1973. This was because the price of raw materials, especially oil, rose much faster than the retail price index we have used. Value added as a result fell well below the 1973 level, so that wages which in 1975 were only about four per cent above the 1973 level took a much higher proportion of value added. Trade unionists must watch very carefully what happens when productivity rises again.

Productivity and Investment

When demand is brisk and lines are being speeded up or manning levels reduced, workers know that productivity must be rising well ahead of earnings. Especially when there are government

Table 18: ICI Expenditure on Fixed Assets and Employment, UK and Overseas, 1966–76

	1966	*1967*	*1968*	*1969*	*1970*	*1971*	*1972*	*1973*	*1974*	*1975*	*1976*
Fixed assets (£m)											
UK	145	81	91	111	118	118	86	80	129	211	268
Overseas	52	33	34	48	64	65	52	40	70	93	170
Total	197	114	125	159	172	183	138	120	199	304	438
Index (1970 = 100)	114	66	73	92	100	106	80	70	116	177	255
Capital goods price index (1970 = 100)	85	86	89	93	100	109	118	138	165	206	240
Volume index	134	77	82	99	100	97	68	51	70	86	106
ICI Employment ('000s) (1970 = 100)											
UK	124	128	139	145	142	137	135	132	132	129	125
Overseas	n.a.	n.a.	48	52	52	53	64	67	69	66	67
Total	n.a.	n.a.	187	197	194	190	199	199	201	195	192

limits on increases in bonus payments, the share of earnings in value added will fall. Profits will therefore rise and that means funds available for investment. The question for trade unionists to raise then is whether such funds have in fact been invested so that new job opportunities are created for the future.

We have seen that productivity may be increased by getting extra output with the same labour or by getting the same output with less labour. It is the last of these two that British industry was getting in the years after 1973. Companies were rationalizing, that is, they were concentrating on their most productive plants and closing down the others. Workers were being laid off. New investment was not being made at a rate that would employ the same number of workers producing a greater output. The chemical industry was no exception. In real terms annual capital investment in the chemical industry fell from around £350m in 1970–1 to about £250m in 1974–5. Employment fell from 440000 to 420000 over the same period. You can find these figures from the annual *Census of Manufacturing*, which also gives the equivalent of value added figures for each industry, under the title of 'Net Output'. What you need to find from your company is the annual figure of capital investment in fixed assets, so that you can follow the changes over the years. Then you can relate these to changes in employment. On the previous page in Table 18 we showed the figures for ICI over the ten years 1966 to 1975.

What we learn from this table is that in real terms capital investment only re-established the level achieved in 1966 ten years later, in 1976. Moreover, the British share of investment at around two-thirds of the total is well below the figure of three-quarters of the total in 1966. The result can be seen in the steady decline in British employment after 1969, only offset by a steady rise in employment overseas. We shall take up this question of transferring assets overseas in Chapter 9.

You will be able to find your company's figures for capital investment in fixed assets and for employment, at least in the UK, in your company's Reports and Accounts over the last few years, so that you can build up a table for your company like Table 18 for ICI (p. 59).

Remember that you will need measures of productivity that will enable the union to bargain about manning and investment.

7. Protecting Jobs Against Redundancy and Bankruptcy

When the Upper Clyde shipyards were being threatened with closure in 1971 a university economist wrote:

The Ridley Report drawn up by the Conservative front bench spokesman on Trade and Industry in 1969 (printed in full in *The Daily Record* for 2nd September 1971), is nothing else but a proposal to devalue UCS's capital for the benefit of any capitalists who are lucky enough to be in a position to come to the market. His proposals include the following (Mr Ridley's words in quotation marks):

(i) to let the Yarrow yard leave UCS (on favourable terms for Yarrow);
(ii) to 'put in a Government "butcher" to cut up UCS and to sell (cheaply) to Lower Clyde (another private yard) and others the assets of UCS' (allegedly to minimise upheaval and dislocation);
(iii) 'after liquidation or reconstruction . . . (to) sell the Government holding in UCS even for a pittance'. (From Robin Murray, *UCS: The Anatomy of Bankruptcy*, Spokesman Books, 1971, p. 31).

We have already seen that jobs may be cut back to increase labour productivity, but they may also be lost when sales decline in a recession or when cash shortages lead to bankruptcy. A company that cannot make ends meet has either to borrow from the banks to tide over the crisis or to go to the Government for help. You need to know what you can do in such circumstances and whether there is a real long-term problem or only a short-term problem. It is always possible that the company you work for is badly managed and has not been producing anything that people want or not investing enough in new equipment to get the price down to a level at which people will buy. It is more than likely, however, that something can be done to rescue the situation without large-scale redundancies or actual bankruptcy.

The important question is whether your firm produces something people want and whether when the recession is over, or when new investment plans mature, people will buy at a price

Clydeside workers ponder their future

that will cover costs. In other words, can the firm be made to work profitably, or, as they say nowadays, is it viable? To answer this question, it is necessary to look at the order books over the last few years and then study the company's capital structure and cash flow.

Order Books

Most order books reveal SEASONAL ups and downs and longer-term CYCLES of ups and downs. If you can discover what these are, you can argue that laying workers off and disbanding a trained labour force may be the worst thing to do. Sales of some products are subject to big seasonal swings, for example sales of toys at Christmas. Others are subject to big cyclical swings. Amounts of sales of capital equipment, including machinery and factory construction, rise up and down in much bigger waves with the cycle of booms and slumps or stagnation than amounts of sales of consumer goods. In either case it should be possible to adopt short-time working or to build up stocks rather than accept redundancy.

Here is an example of steel output in the UK, compared with all manufacturing output in recent industrial cycles. Clearly it would be extremely short-sighted of the steel industry to make massive redundancies in the downturn and then find itself without adequate labour in the upturn. To maintain output it would seem to be sensible to build up stocks, since the years of upturn in the past have often found the steel industry short of supplies.

Table 19: Annual Percentage Changes in Output, UK

	1960	*1961*	*1962*	*1963*	*1964*	*1965*
All industries	+7	+1	+1	+3	+8	+3
Steel industry	+20	−9	−7	+10	+14	+5
	1966	*1967*	*1968*	*1969*	*1970*	
All industries	+1	+1	+5	+3	+1	
Steel industry	−10	−2	+8	+2	+5	
	1971	*1972*	*1973*	*1974*	*1975*	
All industries	0	+3	+7	−4	−5	
Steel industry	−13	+5	+5	−16	−13	

SOURCE: National Institute *Economic Review*.

Steel trade unions have long argued that steel should be stocked in recessions; but of course this means that the Steel Corporation pays out money, for example in wages, with nothing coming in. Money will have to be borrowed and there may be a problem of cash flow.

Capital Structure

Even if order books are well filled for the months and years to come, companies may be faced by problems connected with CAPITAL STRUCTURE as well as with those of cash flow. Both of these problems faced Upper Clyde Shipbuilders in 1971. To start with, UCS had more debts than capital. In 1968 the position was as follows:

Table 20: Upper Clyde Shipbuilders' Capital Structure, 1968 (£m)

Capital issued	5·0
Unsecured loan	0·9
Overdraft	4·2
	10·1
Losses	10·6

In 1969 UCS obtained (in £m):

Loans from Shipbuilding Industry Board and from Government	19·3
But its losses were	12·1

In 1970 the order book stood at £67m but deposits placed with UCS in advance of payments on delivery of ships amounted to only £4m. Trade credit was obtained from the Government up to the limit of £53m. The loss was cut back to £4·1m; but in October the new Conservative Government, following the Ridley Report, withdrew the credit guarantee.

In June 1971 the Government refused a further loan of £6m, although the first half year losses were down to the equivalent of an annual £3·2m and there was every expectation of profits as the ships came off the stocks. The company could not pay its bills and was declared bankrupt.

Any company which lives on credit and overdrafts is in a very precarious position. One murmur – and the Tory Government did more than murmur – that credit guarantees are to be withdrawn, and all creditors will rush in with their bills to get paid before the crash comes. A company must have capital to fall back on. Upper Clyde Shipbuilders was a privately owned company for which the Government provided funds when its losses, as we have seen, were in excess of its capital. The awful warning is there, that if you get Government aid for your company, you must get a capital sum or a grant and not just credit or a guaranteed overdraft, for these can always be cancelled by an unsympathetic subsequent government. Remember that the usual measure of capital structure is to relate:

1. All borrowings, generally including overdrafts along with other loans and fixed interest stocks (that is, those for which fixed payments must be made so long as the company is in business), to
2. Ordinary capital, where dividends depend upon profits.

This is what is called gearing; and it is measured by assuming that no. 2 above is 1 or 100 and showing no. 1 above as a ratio or percentage of no. 2. Shareholders do not want no. 1 to be too high in relation to no. 2, because they do not want too many claims on profits before they get a look in. But for the employees of aided companies the problem of a high gearing of no. 1 to no. 2 is the threat that governments may end credits and overdraft guarantees.

But your company can still have cash flow problems even if its capital structure is quite strong.

Cash Flow

Problems of cash flow can arise whenever a company has large payments to make over a long period of time before it gets back any money from sales. UCS, as we saw, only got £4m in advance payments on orders for £67m of ships. Most companies have various product lines. Some are produced for sale quite quickly; others may require a fairly long period of production, or at least of tooling up for production or of stockbuilding in advance of production. The finance director of a company should have a cash plan of outgoings and incomings; and it should be easy enough for him to see what is happening with the monthly cash movements before him, which he can compare with his own cash plan.

CASH PLANS

On the next page we show what a cash plan looks like to the finance director of a company with four main departments producing different products:

Table 21: A Company's Cash Plan (£m)

	Department / Products								*Total*		*Cumulative balance*
	1		*2*		*3*		*4*				
	In	*Out*	*In*	*Out*	*In*	*Out*	*In*	*Out*	*In*	*Out*	
Year 1											
January	0	2	0	0	4	1	0	0	4	3	+1
February	0	2	0	0	0	1	0	0	0	3	−2
March	2	2	0	0	0	1	0	0	2	3	−3
April	2	2	0	0	0	1	0	0	2	3	−4
May	3	3	0	0	0	1	0	0	3	4	−5
June	3	3	0	2	0	1	0	0	3	6	−8
July	3	3	0	2	4	1	0	0	7	6	−7
August	3	3	0	2	0	1	0	0	3	6	−10
September	3	3	4	2	0	1	0	0	7	6	−9
October	3	3	4	2	0	1	0	0	7	6	−8
November	3	3	4	2	0	1	0	0	7	6	−7
December	3	3	4	2	0	1	0	0	7	6	−6
Total	28	32	16	14	8	12	0	0	52	58	−6
Year 2											
January	3	3	4	2	4	1	0	1	11	7	−2
February	3	3	4	2	0	1	0	1	7	7	−2
March	4	3	4	2	0	1	0	1	8	7	−1
April	4	3	4	3	0	1	5	1	13	8	+4
May	4	3	4	3	0	1	0	1	8	8	+4
June	4	3	4	3	4	1	0	1	12	8	+8
July	4	3	5	3	0	0	0	2	9	8	+9
August	4	3	5	3	0	0	0	2	9	8	+10
September	4	3	5	3	0	0	0	2	9	8	+11
October	4	3	5	4	0	0	0	3	9	10	+10
November	4	4	5	4	0	0	0	3	9	11	+8
December	4	4	5	4	4	0	5	3	18	11	+15
Total	46	38	54	36	12	6	10	21	122	101	+21

NOTE: 'In' figures are for the months' sales receipts.
'Out' figures are for all expenditures in the month.
These include capital expenditures as well as current payments.

This director of finance is having to deal with four products where the profit margin and timing of payments are quite different. The deficits and gains in the balance will not of course necessarily mean losses or profits in the accounts over a particular year, which must also include stock, debtors, creditors, etc.

Look carefully at the columns.

Product no. 1 shows a small deficit on the first year and a small gain on the second year, but in the last two months no gain occurs.

Product no. 2 shows a small gain on the first year and a large gain on the second year,

Product no. 3 is paid for in instalments, which leave a deficit on the first year and a gain on the second,

Product no. 4 is also paid for in instalments; production involves some heavy expenditure before any money comes in and still shows a deficit on the second year.

Taking all the products together, the finance director has a deficit of £6m to face on the first year and a monthly cash deficit from June to December of well over £6m, rising actually to £10m in August. The cash deficit is eliminated by April of the second year and the cash flow is steadily built up over the following months to the overall gain figure of £21m by the end of the second year.

However, it is not difficult to see that any number of unforeseen events could force the finance director's cash plan to go seriously wrong, especially in a period of rising costs.

Firstly, all costs might rise more than anticipated, including interest rates on borrowed money. Unless sales prices are raised in time and in line, most of the margin of profit will disappear. Secondly, it might not be possible to raise sales prices, or prices might actually rise less than budgeted for, and with similar results. Thirdly, credit to cover the big deficits in the middle of the first year might not prove to be available. Fourthly, instalment payments on products nos. 2 and 3 might be delayed because of failure to deliver by contracted dates. Fifthly, the time taken and the cost of building new plant and equipment might increase before the product is available for sale or even for instalment payments to be made. This is often called the GESTATION time, between the drawing-board stage of producing a new car, ship or aeroplane and the delivery of the first production model.

Every single one of these adversities hit Upper Clyde Shipbuilders, and, as we noticed, they had no capital balance to start with but only inherited debts, covered by Government loans and credit guarantees. Yet there seemed to be good reason for supposing that the yards would prove to be profitable in the end. Why did the Government withdraw credit? The argument of the so-called 'Three Wise Men' who were asked to report on UCS was that to provide further credit was throwing good money after bad. Already too much credit had been given to this 'lame duck'. A newly elected Conservative Government evidently wished to show that it was in earnest about giving no feather beds to ailing public enterprise. But there is more to bankruptcy than this. The results of a bankruptcy provide an extremely important insight into the way in which capitalism works.

Liquidation

Why should owners of capital want to close down a company, when it might become profitable or is still just profitable? We saw in the last chapter that giant companies like ICI might wish to reduce investment and employment in the UK and expand overseas; or they might just wish to rationalize their total operations so as to produce the same or less output with even fewer workers. It might be more profitable for them to do this, especially if the market in the UK was not growing. They might make more money by lending their money to the Government at high interest rates, as GEC was doing in 1974–6, than by investing in new plant. Companies are in business to make profits, not to provide employment. But in addition to all this there are special advantages for owners of capital from forcing a liquidation. Some capitalists, the owners of the liquidated company, will suffer; but others, those who buy up the assets, will gain. The new owners of Rolls-Royce Motors are doing fine, because they have nothing to pay to the old owners since the old company went bankrupt and they got the motorcar business assets and goodwill for a song.

What happens in a bankruptcy, that is a situation where a company has not the cash to pay its bills, is that a LIQUIDATOR is appointed. His job is to dispose of the assets for cash as best he can and divide up the money realized in this way among the creditors. Bank overdrafts and mortgages have to be settled first. We shall say more about this in the next chapter. Assets will consist of buildings, plant and equipment, vehicles, stock, etc., and any debts owing from debtors to the company.

Now in the case of UCS there was a special feature. Most of

the creditors were public sector suppliers, the Post Office, Electricity and Gas Boards, etc., and the British Steel Corporation above all. Some were foreign companies; they also suffered. The result of the liquidation of a company is not only that its owners and the creditors lose money; there are gainers also. These are the buyers of the buildings, plant and equipment, etc., that are sold off by the liquidator to pay what he can to the creditors. Valuable items often go at knockdown bargain prices for two reasons: first, the liquidator is in a hurry and cannot wait for a more favourable price; second, plant and equipment often have a certain value as a total productive unit, but much less in the open market as bits and pieces for other uses.

In this table, the figures for the Upper Clyde Shipbuilders' liquidation tell the story.

Table 22: Assets of Upper Clyde Shipbuilders (£m)

	1968	*1971 Book value*	*1971 Liquidator's estimated realizable value*
Fixed assets			
Land, buildings	5·8	2·5	2·1
Plant, equipment	3·5	4·1	1·0
Total	9·3	6·6	3·1
Goodwill[1]	1·2		
Current Assets			
Stocks, work in progress	7·9[2]	0·35	0·25
Debtors[3]	5·3[3]	0·34	0·34
Grants from SIB[4]	5·5	—	—
Cash, etc.	0·5	—	—
Total	19·2	0·69	0·59
All Assets	29·7	7·29	3·69

NOTES:

1. The goodwill was that of the Yarrow yard (see p. 70).
2. Mainly ships. 3. Includes bad debts.
4. Shipbuilding Industry Board.

SOURCE: Robin Murray, *UCS: The Anatomy of Bankruptcy*. Spokesman Books, 1971.

The figures look rather worse than normal, because the value of ships being built (most of the stocks and work in progress) in this case belonged to the customers, the shipowners. There is also the fact that the Government sold off the Yarrow yard of UCS to Yarrow and Co. Ltd at a loss overall to UCS, according to the liquidator, of £1·7m.

Taking into account the Government funds put into UCS, amounting to some £24m (£6·5m in grants, the rest in loans), and assuming the liquidator did better than he expected, as indeed he did, and raised more than £5m from liquidation, what happened was that the Government, not to mention the public corporations, lost at least £19m on the bankruptcy. Yarrow and Co. and the purchasers of the plant, buildings and equipment were the gainers. In fact, the companies succeeding UCS, Govan Shipbuilders (a state-owned company) and Marathon, paid £2·5m and £1·5m respectively for the sites and the plant that was not auctioned. A bankruptcy destroys old capital and restructures it under new management. This is often described as the sanitary system of capitalism. In the process, the labour force is dismissed and re-engaged – in the old days at lower rates. Today the rates are better, but less than two-thirds of the 1968 UCS labour force is employed in Govan, Marathon and Yarrow, that is, 6000 instead of 10000 men. Had it not been for the struggle of the UCS workers to retain their jobs and keep all the yards in operation, still more men could have been rendered unemployed and an even lower price realized for the assets. The costs and benefits to society are not taken into account in a liquidation, but only the costs and benefits to owners of capital. We look at this further in Chapter 10.

Cash Ratios

Let us now go back to our finance director's cash plan. Without access to this inside information, is there any way in which it is possible to tell the cash position or liquidity of a company? There is nothing as definite as a published monthly cash statement. To reveal such secrets would be regarded as unnecessarily risking loss of confidence among shareholders and bankers, if the position looks bad, and gratuitously encouraging union negotiators to ask for more, if the position looks good. There are, however, some important indicators in the annual accounts; and some companies publish half-yearly and even quarterly statements. The place to look is in the current assets and current liabilities.

Remember that the current assets include stocks, debtors, short-term loans (to others) and bank balances. Current liabilities include overdrafts, short-term loans (received), trade bills, creditors, taxes and dividends payable. If current assets exceed current liabilities, then all should be well in the long run for the company. However, stocks may be a large item in the assets and these may not be so easy to change into cash (to liquidate) as other assets. So you can work out two ratios:

$$\text{the current ratio} = \frac{\text{current assets}}{\text{current liabilities}}$$

$$\text{the quick ratio} = \frac{\text{current assets less stocks}}{\text{current liabilities}}$$

One other clue to cash flow can be found by looking at the size of the outstanding debts in relation to sales and thinking of this as so many days per year, over which debts would have to be collected from sales. This ratio is:

$$\text{the debt collection period in days per year} = \frac{\text{debtors} \times 365}{\text{sales}}$$

Now you should be able to work out these ratios from the accounts of the company you work for, and decide how well placed it is for cash and survival.

But these ratios are not just of academic interest. They are part of the information and control system of any large organization. If you are going to make use of them you will need to have them broken down to the level of the organization that is relevant for your purposes; and you will need to relate them to the overall policy on redundancy your union is pursuing.

8. Controlling Rationalization: Planning Against Closures

A Boardroom Battle

'It's a carve-up,' the shop stewards said. 'They're after stripping the assets and sacking half the employees.' Plants can be closed for other reasons than falling sales, cash flow problems and bankruptcy. Many of the closures in the late 1960s and early 1970s were the results of RATIONALIZATION in mergers and takeovers. What this meant was that smaller firms and less profitable operations were closed down, not because they were losing money, but because they weren't making as much money as another, probably larger, company thought that it could make using just some of the assets and taking over all the customers.

This was the remarkable example that came my way in 1973. The Combined Shop Stewards' Committee at Thomas Firth and John Brown's Group, a world-famous Sheffield firm of special steel-makers, asked for help in preparing their case against a threatened takeover. There were two bidders for the group: a rival Sheffield firm called Dunford and Elliott, and a Manchester wire-making group called Johnson and Nephew, which was a subsidiary, and in this case purely a vehicle, for Oliver Jessel's giant CONGLOMERATE finance company, Jessel Securities. He was known to have interests in other Sheffield special steel-making companies and there had been much talk of rationalization. The board of Firth Brown's had rejected the Dunford and Elliott offer and was recommending its shareholders to accept a £32m takeover by Jessel. The shop stewards wanted to know what the chances were of going it alone until a Labour Government was returned to office and nationalized special steel-making. In the meantime, the stewards warned both bidders that no work would leave the factories unless the jobs of all 7000 workers were guaranteed.

SHOP STEWARDS DEMAND PROBE INTO TAKEOVER

Mr OLIVER JESSEL
"Storm in a teacup."

Carve-up fears at Firth Brown

By FRAZER WRIGHT
Industrial Correspondent

Firth and Brown group shop stewards last night demanded Government and Stock Exchange inquiries into the secret background to big money bidding for their group by financier Oliver Jessel, and Sheffield steel group Dunford and Elliott.

They want a full investigation into what they claim have been secret attempts by Mr Jessel to get unopposed control of the company "and then carve it up" with Dunford and Elliott, said Firth and Brown convenor Mr Richard Caborn.

Dunfords last night claimed that approaches had been made, but said they had turned them down flat. Mr Jessel said: "I have nothing whatsoever to hide. I would welcome an investigation. This is a storm in a teacup."

Mr Caborn said stewards had written evidence from Dunfords of the approaches by Mr Jessel — with a view to D and E dropping out of the takeover battle, and leaving the field clear for his subsidiary, Richard Johnson and Nephew.

Urgency

But Mr Jessel, in a letter read to stewards by the Firth and Brown directors yesterday, denied the allegations, claiming the approach had come from Dunfords.

According to the stewards, such talks could have involved the carve-up of the big steel group, and the floating off of sections of it by Mr Jessel.

"More evidence keeps coming out to indicate that there is going to be a carve-up of Firth and Brown," said Mr Caborn. Now stewards wanted the whole question of the future of the 7,000-employee group to be examined in the light of the takeover activities."

They will be asking MPs from areas, with Firth and Brown plants to raise the takeover in Parliament as a matter of urgency. The stewards also want the allegations over the secret approaches to be studied by the Stock Exchange Takeover Panel.

Both sides should be examined, said Mr Caborn. "I don't think Dunford and Elliott are lilywhite," he said.

The Government inquiry into the matter, said Mr Caborn, should concentrate both on the conduct of the takeover and the question of security of employment at Firth and Brown works, whichever bid is successful.

Mr RICHARD CABORN
"Evidence keeps coming out."

Mr PETER EDWARDS
"Absolute nonsense"

The workers in the Firth Brown plants are being given detailed breakdowns of the stewards' fact-finding in a special leaflet. This also calls for a two-hour stoppage of work at all plants when the eventual takeover comes for mass meetings.

This latest bombshell in what is already Sheffield's most controversial takeover deal came after an icy meeting between the stewards and their own directors, who have backed the £33m Jessel bid.

The meeting covered the stewards' claims about the secret approaches, and Mr Caborn said that the Firth Brown directors would now have to give the matter serious consideration.

Again, the stewards emphasised their fight to retain an independent Firth and Brown group, and, said Mr Caborn, they submitted their evidence over the Jessel approaches. This was met by the letter from Mr Jessel.

Two approaches had been made, said Mr Caborn, one before the RJN bid.

Last night, Mr Peter Edwards, a director of Dunford and Elliott, and their top Sheffield steelman said it was "absolute nonsense" to claim that his group made the first move over any carve-up.

"There were approaches made by representatives of Mr Jessel to our merchant

TURN to BACK PAGE

When we looked at the accounts we could see clearly enough what the bidders were after:

1. The GOODWILL, in this case the customers of the recently acquired British Steel Corporation's business in medium-sized open die alloy forgings, which had been obtained from BSC in part-exchange for the flat product side of Firth Vickers' Stainless Steel Co., previously a part of Firth Brown's;

2. The company's high current ratio and its incredibly strong cash position, a nest egg of over £6m cash, of particular value when pressure on cash flow was general;

3. Independence from the PRICE LEADERSHIP of BSC in nearly all of the company's products, and, which was particularly valuable in a year of Government price control on the home market, a sizeable proportion of the company's total sales were in the export market;

4. A capital investment programme of £10m, authorized and in part committed in the previous two years for a melting shop, electro-slag remelting plant and the River Don Stampings, the benefits of which would be appearing in the next year or two;

5. A high level of research and development expenditure, which was the basis of several new advances in steel technology, in which the company had a monopoly.

At the same time the stewards were not convinced that the £6m cash would be spent on investing in new plant to ensure employment for their members. Jessel had other interests, in property, insurance and commodities here and abroad. It seemed well worth fighting him and trying to get the company to fend off both bidders and go it alone. This seemed more feasible when rumours circulated in the City columns of the national press that City finance was available in a plan to strengthen the company's capital structure. The great day was going to be 2 March 1973 when the chairman of Firth Brown's, himself a city merchant banker from Hambros Bank, would announce the board's proposals at the company's annual general meeting. The Stewards' Committee had for some years held three separate shares in the company in order to receive all communications to shareholders. (I attended as PROXY for one of these stewards, much to the alarm of the company secretary who informed me that I had no right to speak, although the nominee shareholders had proxies and could speak.)

The annual general meeting turned out to be a stand-up argument between the shop stewards' convenor and the company chairman. He would only say that there *had* been a plan for going it alone but the chances of success did not look good enough. The convenor asked how good they were; the chances of success of conglomerate takeovers had just been revealed in a *Bank Review* article as about 1 in 3. No answer. Most of the shareholders attending the meeting appeared to be drawn from present and past members of the company's management. We were provided with a retired managing director making the surprising statement that he had never thought he would live to find himself wholly in agreement with the company's shop stewards against the views of the board of directors. The real powers behind the throne remained silent. This company was one of those where the majority shareholding was in the hands of what are called 'bank nominee companies'. These are a cover for institutions like insurance companies, but also for individuals who do not want their identities to be revealed. Rarely but occasionally they may conceal the direct interest of a bank. The argument tailed off and a sycophant from the floor called for a vote of thanks to the chairman and directors. He did not even get a seconder; and rather sheepishly the chairman closed the meeting.

You may say that the shop stewards' protest made little difference, but in the next few weeks the battle raged. Dunford and Elliott raised their bid and Jessel trumped it. The Combined Stewards' Committee issued a stern warning to the management of the company with copies circulated to every worker: 'that in the event of a take-over materialising, no finished work will leave the factories. This will continue until any new management give assurances that the jobs of the work-force (staff and manual) are secure.' On 2 April the shop stewards' convenor received a letter from Oliver Jessel guaranteeing that there would be no redundancies as a result of the merger.

Some may say that it didn't matter what the books said; the threat of action was the thing. But understanding the books undoubtedly strengthened the stewards' confidence; and explaining what was in them had given confidence also to the workers that their stewards should be supported. The threat had to be credible; the stewards' knowledge made it so. Within eighteen months the Jessel empire crashed and Firth Brown was set to pass into state hands. But the EEC ruled against this and a group of City institutions headed by Hambros Bank, be it noted, bought up the Jessel shares in the joint Johnson and Firth Brown group of companies. What is perhaps more, when Jessel Securities crashed and Firth Brown came up for a second takeover, the shop stewards demanded a revised management structure which included the demand for a large element of worker control at all levels. The lessons learnt in the earlier takeover bid were being put into practice.

The Firth Brown shop stewards got their information from the Annual Report and Accounts. Limited though these may be, they can be very useful. Here is another case to look at, where stewards would have been helped by using one of the regular Stock Exchange information services such as Extel.

Imperial Typewriters' Closure

On 17 January 1975 Litton Industries, a giant American conglomerate corporation, announced that its two subsidiary plants in Britain manufacturing Imperial typewriters would be closed as from 21 February and production transferred to their West German subsidiary, Triumph-Adler. There had been no prior consultation with the unions representing the 3200 workers at the Hull and Leicester plants. Examination of Litton's accounts and statements in 1974 could have alerted shop stewards in the English subsidiary that there was a possible threat to its survival. It had been reported for some time that the English operations had been running at a loss (which turned out to have totalled £5m over 1972–3 and 1973–4); and in September 1974 Litton had announced a $40m loss for the whole conglomerate, 'resulting from a $77m reserve set up for operations to be discontinued'. As the *Financial Times* put it, this was 'the typewriting on the wall'.

How to Read an Extel Card

Here is what the Extel card looked like for 6 September 1974. First look at the share price ups and down on the graph which shows a fall from 98·7 high for a one dollar share in 1967 to a low of 6·0 in 1974. Then look at the two main blocks of figures in the middle (figures for 1974 and 1975 are in italics because they are estimates); the first section is for sales and income (earnings) *per share*; the second is for sales and income, etc., in millions of dollars ($). In the first section sales per share, cash flow, capital spending, book value move up and down and up again, but earnings per share and average annual P/E (Price/Earnings) ratio moves steadily down after 1967–8, with an actual loss shown by a little 'd' for deficit in 1972 and in 1974. In 1973 the average price of each share was about 9·0 (between 13·2 and 6·1), while earnings per share were 0·96;

$$\frac{0{\cdot}96\times100}{9{\cdot}0}=10{\cdot}7$$

If the same figures are compared according to British practice to show earnings YIELD, the calculation is:

$$\frac{9{\cdot}0}{0{\cdot}96}=9{\cdot}4$$

What these comparisons tell us is the return that buyers of shares can expect to get on their money. They pay $9 for a share and get $0·96 income (not necessarily all paid as a dividend now),

TON INDUSTRIES NYSE-LIT RECENT PRICE 6.0 DIV'D YIELD Nil (NORM Nil) P/E RATIO 5.4

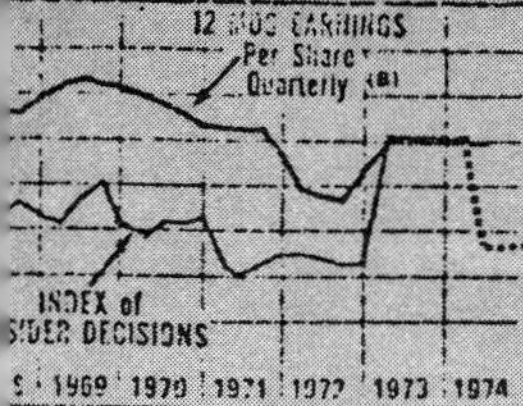

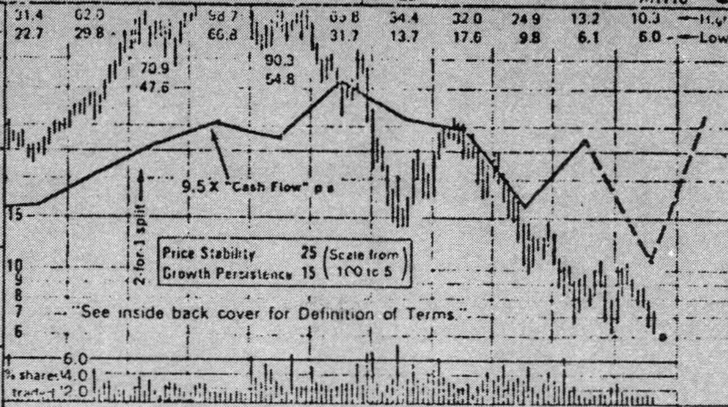

ares Held by Investment Companies

'73	9/30/73	12/31/73	3/31/74
02	102,460	102,460	122,460
ds)	(2 funds)	(2 funds)	(3 funds)

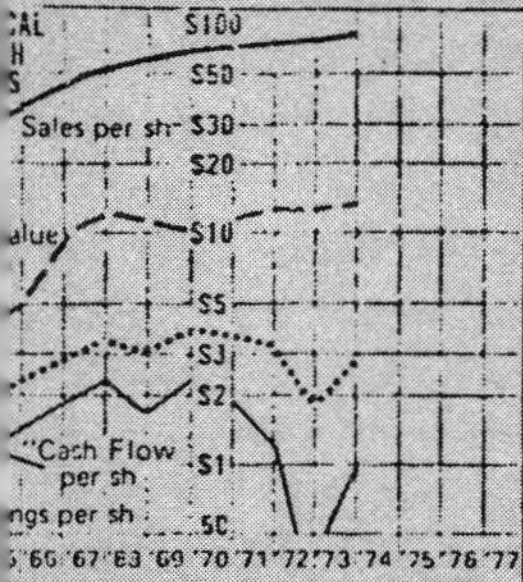

1964	1965	1966	1967	1968	1969	1970	1971	1972	1973	1974	1975	
25.49	33.50	39.96	48.97	52.55	73.39	66.44	68.02	67.96	66.93	85.35	88.75 (A)	Sal
1.71	2.22	2.78	3.25	2.89	4.46	3.42	3.13	1.74	2.81	1.15	3.45	"C
1.08	1.38	1.88	2.19	1.62	2.62	1.73	1.21	d.23	.96	d1.30	1.15	Ea
1.08	1.38	1.85	2.19	1.58	2.15	1.72	1.21	d.23	.99	d1.30	1.15 (B)	Eg
--	--	--	--	--	--	--	--	--	--	Nil	Nil (C)	Div
1.32	1.83	2.08	1.90	2.71	5.70	4.29	2.35	2.25	1.75	2.45	2.00	Ca
3.83	4.58	9.01	11.80	11.31	8.00	11.24	12.32	12.09	13.04	12.70	15.35	Bo
26.92	27.33	29.34	31.69	35.30	29.66	36.19	36.26	36.44	36.87	35.50	35.75 (D)	Co
25.8	29.3	28.5	34.5	46.6	25.9	17.0	20.7	--	10.7	--		Av
--	--	--	--	--	--	--	--	--	--	--		Av
685.1	915.6	1172.2	1561.5	1855.0	2175.6	2404.3	2466.1	2476.6	2467.9	3029	3150 (A)	Sal
11.5%	11.2%	11.3%	10.5%	8.7%	9.7%	9.3%	8.2%	4.9%	8.0%	--	7.2%	Op
16.8	23.0	26.6	33.8	44.9	54.7	61.1	69.7	71.8	68.2	78.0	82.0	De
29.8	39.8	55.6	70.1	58.5	82.3	68.8	50.0	d2.3	41.6	d39.8	46.7	Ne
9.6%	9.3%	9.6%	9.3%	8.9%	8.1%	7.6%	8.2%	8.1%	8.2%	8.1%	8.1%	De
47.0%	44.3%	42.2%	41.6%	42.5%	37.5%	42.3%	41.0%	47.5%	45.3%	--	45.0%	Inc
4.3%	4.4%	4.7%	4.5%	3.2%	3.8%	2.9%	2.0%	NMF	1.7%	--	1.5%	Ne
146.9	184.3	203.1	241.1	252.8	273.2	439.5	443.8	446.8	410.5	410	440	Fu
149.5	214.0	281.1	389.1	550.3	593.8	647.4	667.4	681.3	721.7	670	715	Ne
198.3	235.7	320.4	401.4	457.4	501.3	653.0	712.2	711.8	763.3	800	870	Wo
12.0%	12.0%	13.2%	12.9%	8.8%	11.0%	8.6%	6.8%	2.2%	5.9%	--	7.0%	%
19.9%	18.6%	19.8%	18.0%	10.5%	13.9%	10.6%	7.3%	NMF	5.8%	--	7.0%	%
2%	5%	1%	1%	2%	6%	9%	12%	--	15%	NMF	13%	%

RATES (per sh)	Past 10 Yrs	Past 5 Yrs	Est '71-'73 to '77-'79
	16.0%	8.0%	5.5%
Flow"	10.5%	−2.5%	7.5%
gs	0.5%	−19.0%	16.5%
alue	13.5%	3.5%	7.0%

POSITION (ll.)	1971	1972	7/31/73
ssets	90.0	92.7	85.7
ables	598.9	559.2	659.7
ries	531.2	645.1	680.9
	18.2	20.3	16.4
Assets	1238.3	1317.3	1442.7
ayable	221.4	227.7	341.3
ue	212.1	285.1	240.7
	92.6	92.7	97.3
Liab'ties	526.1	605.5	679.3

STRUCTURE as of 7/31/73
$410.5 mill. Interest $27.6 mill.
7.2 mill. 3 1/2% 1987 conv. at $42.50
$0.6 mill. 5 1/4% 12/74 conv. at $20.
Uncapitalized: annual rentals about
6 mill. Pension Liab'ty None
$240.8 mill. Pfd Div. $6.1 mill.
shs. Series A $3 cum. pfd. conv. into
com.; 2,880,000 shs. Series B cum. pfd.
to .14 shs. com.
Stock 34,541,834 average shares
as of 10/31/73
31 shs. cum. part. pref. ea. conv. to
shs. com., conv. rate increases by
annually to 1989.

QUARTERLY SALES ($ Millions) Oct. 31	Jan. 31	Apr. 30	July 31	(A) Full Fiscal Year
565.0	599.6	619.5	682.0	2466.1
582.2	622.3	675.7	596.4	2476.6
582.5	597.8	632.7	654.9	2467.9
677.8	736.3	819.0	795.9	3029
730	790	850	770	3150

EARNINGS AS REPORTED (per sh) Oct. 31	Jan. 31	Apr. 30	July 31	(B) Full Fiscal Year
.29	.29	.30	.33	1.21
.29	d.29	d.43	.20	d.23
.23	.25	.22	.29	.99
.27	.29	.23	d2.09	d1.30
.23	.30	.25	.32	1.15

QUARTERLY DIVIDENDS PAID Mar. 31	June 30	Sept. 30	Dec. 31	(C) Full Year
NO DIVIDENDS BEING PAID				

BUSINESS: Litton Industries, Inc., derived about half its growth from acquisitions. Business products (from machinery to paper forms) account for 38% of revenues; defense equipment (from Naval vessels to electronic systems), 24%; industrial equipment (from machine tools to electric motors), 23%; and professional products (from X-ray machines to publication... puchases account for 22% o... shareholders. 105,400 e... control 5% of common. 11%... Chairman: C.B. Thornton. ... Inc.: Delaware. Address: 3... Beverly Hills, Calif. 90210.

Litton shares are for the patient investor. Since our June review, the stock's Performance rank has dropped to 3 (Average). The company has just announced a $39.8 million loss for fiscal 1974, resulting from a $77.2 million reserve set up for operations to be discontinued. When full details are released, we will issue a Supplementary Report.

A $250 million revolving credit agreement has been concluded with a consortium of 15 lending banks headed by Wells Fargo and Morgan Guaranty Trust Company. The agreement provides for an initial 5-year term loan of $100 million and a 3-year revolving credit of $150 million that is convertible at any time into 4-year term borrowings. The term loan will be used to retire outstanding short-term bank debt. The revolving credit will be available for general corporate purposes.

Erie Marine has been closed. Since negotiations with Bethlehem Steel for the construction of three ore carriers were ter-

cost of $20 million in 1969

The LHA dispute seems important part of the ... operations is tied to the ... Navy to produce 30 DD-9... and 5 LHA general pu... assault vessels. Pursuant ... Litton's shipbuilding divi... $3 billion of work to com... hitch, however, is that ... original pricing schedule ... cover later cost increases. ... stands to sustain a sizab... Navy agrees to pay ... proposal was submitted b... 1972, but as yet the Navy ... tention of easing the com... Litton's contention that ... resulted from post-contra... by the Navy, for which ad... tion should be forthcomi...

CASH POSITION
Current Assets to Current Liabilities

that is 10·7 per cent return. They can compare that with the rates of return from other investments. As income goes down, the share price will go down. If income goes up, the price will go up.

In the second section we can see that, while sales were increasing in value, the operating margins were falling all the time and especially as net income fell after 1969. Depreciation was increasing but not in relation to sales (Depreciation rate). The income tax rate changed little. What was going wrong was that, while corporate net worth was steadily increasing, including working capital (that is net current assets), net income was not rising but falling. The graphs on the left illustrate the figures. Companies were being bought up to increase the net worth of the fixed and current assets of the corporation, but they were not earning more for the corporation shareholders. Interest on debt and preferred dividends were taking $34m. The per cent earned to net worth, that is the net income as a percentage of net worth, was falling to the 1974 figure:

$$\frac{41{\cdot}6}{721{\cdot}7} \times 100 = 5{\cdot}8$$

In 1974 Litton announced (see lower half of the card in the middle) a loss of $39·8m 'resulting from a $77·2 million reserve set up for operations to be discontinued'.

If the shop stewards in Hull and Leicester had spotted that warning in September 1974, they could have prepared for January 1975. As it was, when the closure was announced the Imperial workers in Hull decided with the help of their union, the Transport and General, to form a Union Action Committee, to occupy the plant and appeal to the Government for financial aid, to 'maintain production and/or establish a Cooperative to assume ownership and management of the plant'. In a detailed statement, 'Why Imperial Typewriters MUST NOT Close' (Pamphlet No. 46 published by the Institute for Workers Control), the Action Committee had revealed that the £9·5m investment by Litton in Imperial after 1971 had consisted of equipment transferred to Hull from the Royal Typewriter plant in the US (which had been closed because it could not compete with foreign imports), and that the bulk of the English output had then been steadily exported to the US. So they made an examination of the UK Trade and Navigation Accounts. These showed that not only Imperial's output but most of the UK output in typewriters was being exported, since it was at the lower end of the product range, technologically less advanced than that required in the UK market, which was in turn largely supplied by imports. The Action Committee wanted to know why Litton had not invested in more advanced production methods in Britain and what had been their pricing policy in selling English-made old-fashioned typewriters back to the US. Litton Industries is one of the top fifty US trans-nationally operating corporations, although its UK operations were relatively small.

The Imperial closure thus provides a perfect example of the

reasoning behind the Labour Government's proposal in the 1975 Industry Act for reaching planning agreements with 'major and strategic firms in key sectors of manufacturing industry and selected industries other than manufacturing of particular importance to the economy. Multinational companies will be included only in respect of their British holdings.' This is quoted from the Labour Government 1974 White Paper, 'The Regeneration of British Industry', which formed the basis for the 1975 Industry Act. The British management of Litton Industries had decided in 1974 not to appeal to the British Government for funds to continue their operations in Britain; Litton had already received regional and other investment grants from the Government, since Humberside was designated as a grey area in 1971 and unemployment in Hull was well above the national average. The proposal for planning agreements was designed to reveal to trade unions what was happening in their companies and to help the Government to plan for other investments to sustain full employment in just such circumstances.

More than ever, what matters here is who is going to use the information and at what level of the organization – unit, plant, division, company, combine, national board, international holding company. You may have to pool the information available at different levels of your union organization and you will want advance information of plans as well as data on past and current activities.

9. Checking on Those Hidden Transfers to Accounts Overseas

When the stewards challenged the closure of Imperial Typewriters, they argued that no money had been invested in new plant; in fact new plant had been bought with Government aid but never used. Losses were due to declining sales of an old-fashioned model manufactured with clapped-out equipment, while new models were being developed in West Germany with new equipment. But losses in one country can also be created in a trans-national company by the way the prices are fixed for parts that are moved from a factory in one country to an associated factory in another. This is called transfer pricing; it applies equally to transfers between plants and departments in the same country and to transfers between plants in different countries.

Why Chrysler (UK) Lost Money

In 1970 the Chrysler Motor Corporation of the USA took over Rootes Motors. This was after a £9 million loss by Rootes in 1969 and another £10 million loss in 1970. Three years of profitable operation followed, but in 1974 losses were £11 million, in 1975 double that figure and in 1976 losses of £40 million were expected. Chrysler decided to pull out of the UK and offered the Government the assets valued at £85 million for £35 million, but without the Chrysler sales organization. The Government at first rejected the offer and proposed phasing out the 25000 workers involved, because the car industry already had 25 per cent excess capacity in the UK. After much negotiation, it finally provided Chrysler with £72·5 million guarantees against losses over the four years 1976–9 and with £90 million in loans to continue operating with a reduced manpower of about 15000. There was much discussion about whether this was sensible in view of the Government's £1300 million commitment to British Leyland and the very limited commitment of some £30 million from Chrysler

towards future losses and new investment. What was not discussed was the cause of the huge and growing Chrysler losses.

Here are some figures, revealed by the Labour Research Department in June 1975, from the Society of Motor Manufacturers and Traders' publications and from the Annual Reports of the four big motorcar manufacturers in the UK. Note that this was four months before the chairman of Chrysler announced plans for disposing of its British operations.

Table 23: How Motorcar Prices Were Fixed, 1974

Company	*Average price per vehicle* (£) *Sold in UK*	*Exported from UK*	*Trading profit or loss per vehicle* (£)	*Notes*
Chrysler	1620	629	−21	Includes exported kits
BL	1750	1248	+60	Includes exported kits
Ford	1550	2035	+103	Includes exported engines
Vauxhall	n.a.	1184	+68	1973 figures

SOURCE: Labour Research Department, *Fact Service*, 28 June 1975. It could be that Chrysler exported its cheaper models and that it exported many more kits than the other companies; but the export value per car does seem surprisingly low. If this was artificially fixed at that low level, it could have been done deliberately because Chrysler wanted to make a loss in the UK for one or more of these reasons:

1. To shift funds from the UK for investment in new plant elsewhere;
2. To avoid the higher rates of company tax in Britain;
3. To get Government aid to the tune of £162·5m (which is what they got);
4. To reduce employment by 8000 out of 25000 British jobs without arousing too much opposition.

The Labour Research Department added one further piece of information, that since 1968 Chrysler cars have all been sold through Chrysler International SA, a subsidiary registered in Switzerland where taxes on company profits are only 10 per cent, one third of the UK rate. LRD complain that the last set of accounts of the Swiss company were for 1969, when the trading profit was £12m or double the UK profit at the same date.

In 1972 the chairman of another trans-national motorcar company, Henry Ford II, recommended against a £30m investment in the UK because the 'country was constantly dogged with labour problems'. That year Ford investment as a percentage of sales was cut in the UK: it was 9·7 in 1970 and 7·4 in 1971; then it was 3·9 in 1972 and 4·3 in 1973. The average for all areas of Ford's operations was 5·7 and 6·4 in 1972 and 1973. These figures come from a study made in 1974 by the International Metalworkers' Federation of the Ford Motor Company's corporate strategy.

When you look at your own company, this ratio of investment to sales for different areas is a key statistic. As the TUC *Economic Review* for 1976 (p. 61) commented: 'Only when agreed policies on issues such as investment and tax incentives, minimum industrial relations standards, information disclosure and capital flows are applied by all governments on an international basis will multi-national companies' powers of blackmail be controlled.'

The TUC had already suggested in its *Economic Review* for 1975 that:

> one major step would be the tightening up of company law in Britain so that the global parent accounts of multi-nationals operating in Britain must be filed with the Registrar of Companies according to UK accounting conventions; a global breakdown of employment on a country by country basis would be filed; and all transactions with the affiliates, whether on capital or revenue account, would be separately disclosed.

Planning Agreements under the 1975 Industry Act

One of the main aims of these planning agreements as indicated in the Government White Paper, 'The Regeneration of British Industry', was that information should be made available to Government and unions so that some control could be exercised over the plans of the giant trans-national companies. The Industry Act, like the Employment Protection Act we looked at in Chapter 3, allowed that some information might be secret if disclosure was against the national interest (as with defence secrets), if information had been obtained confidentially (as in the case of personal information about employees), or if disclosure 'might be seriously prejudicial to the interests of the undertaking' (as in the case of secret processes and knowledge which give companies a monopoly, or of financial difficulties which might lead to speculation).

These are not considerations likely to be essential in order to reach planning agreements. How sensitive this information is thought to be, however, can be seen from the amendments made to the Industry Bill as it passed through the House of Commons. These included the following:

1. A trade union that wants the Act to be used to get information has to persuade the Minister to act;

2. The Minister cannot make a compulsory order unless he has given the company at least three months' notice;

3. The company can choose the trade union representative to whom it gives information;

4. The company can object to passing information to trade unions, not only on grounds of secrecy but on the general ground that it 'would cause substantial injury to the undertaking'. (Trade unions can appeal to an independent committee against a decision not to reveal information, but the Minister will have the power to overrule the committee's decision.)

Trade unions may be better advised to use Section 17 of the Employment Protection Act which states that employers must reveal information 'without which trade union representatives would be to a material extent impeded' in collective bargaining, and in addition employers must release information which it would be 'good industrial practice' to disclose.

ACAS has issued a code of practice to define this vague phrase, but employers will not be required to release any document or allow trade unionists to inspect any document.

In the meantime here is the list of information that may be required under the Industry Act, Part IV, Section 30 (2):

(a) the persons employed in the undertaking, or persons normally so employed (but not specifically as to individuals);
(b) the undertaking's capital expenditure;
(c) fixed capital assets used in the undertaking;
(d) any disposal or intended disposal of such assets;
(e) any acquisition or intended acquisition of fixed capital assets for use in the undertaking;
(f) the productive capacity and capacity utilisation of the undertaking;
(g) the undertaking's output and productivity;
(h) sales of the undertaking's products;
(i) exports of those products by the undertaking;
(j) sales of industrial or intellectual property owned or used in connection with the undertaking, grants of rights in respect of such property, and contracts for any such sales or grants; and
(k) expenditure on any research or development programme.

International Agreements

What about the company that is concealing its investment plans behind the manipulation of transfer prices?

The TUC recognizes that:

There are difficulties in extending Planning Agreements beyond the bounds of national sovereignty to the overseas operations of even British-based multinationals. Because of such difficulties the TUC also recognises the urgent need for international intergovernmental regulation. The ultimate aim is a comprehensive General Agreement on Multinational Corporations.

The TUC goes on to 'urge the Government to take the lead internationally in implementation of such progressive measures' as have already been suggested in United Nations reports.

These measures included:

the prevention of investment in countries where workers' rights are not respected; the international levelling-up of, and bargaining on, health and safety standards; the removal of restrictions on expressions of international labour solidarity; the prevention of political interference by multi-nationals; the establishment of a UN Commission on multinationals.

Trade union representatives in trans-national companies have supported these proposals but have not wanted to wait for such agreements to be reached. A combination of regional and national agreements, plant or company bargaining and co-ordinated bargaining right across the plants of the trans-national companies has been the aim of Charles Levinson, secretary general of the International Chemical Workers' Federation. The advantage of combining regional, national and company action is that the information obtained from national statistics, for example on the value of imports and exports of specific goods, can be checked against the shop-floor knowledge of trade unionists. If the customs declarations of the companies show figures like those in the table at the head of this chapter (p. 83), you will know if you work for Chrysler which models are exported and what proportion is in kits and whether, from the point of view of quality, the value of exports should be lower than that of home sales.

The main development of Levinson's strategy so far has been the meetings of trade union representatives and combine committees for particular companies. The most spectacular have been the successful collaboration between shop stewards of Dunlop in Southampton and Pirelli of Milan, which is well known, and the Michelin World Trade Union Council, set up in 1971.

DPN dunlop pirelli

NOTIZIE/NEWS

DUNLOP-PIRELLI INTERNATIONAL SHOP STEWARDS STEERING COMMITTEE | SPECIAL EDITION No. 1

June 9th: international day of action and solidarity

Since the announcement of the merger two years ago, over 8,000 Dunlop-Pirelli workers in the U.K. have lost their jobs and one factory — St. Mary Mills — has been closed down; in Italy 1,000 have been made redundant at Bicocca (Milan) and another factory — SAPSA — has been run down.

Nor do we have any optimism that the list of redundacies in Italy is now closed. From many sources — including the authoritative British business periodical, "The Investors Chronicle" — we hear that in order to complete its rationalisation programme *the way it wants to*, Pirelli needs more redundancies, which up to now "the Italian unions have stood in the way of."

So we must always be on our toes. And don't forget that if Pirelli has difficulty getting the redundancies it wants in Italy, — it may well try elsewhere: Burton? Carlisle? in Spain? in Germany? Wherever it is, we must stand together and fight. There's no other language they understand.

Pirelli workers demonstrating in the centre of Milan against redundancies and short-time working following the Dunlop-Pirelli merger. (Photo on page three shows a D-P shop stewards meeting in Milan in September 1971. The British stewards are seated around the table)

DUNLOP-PIRELLI

Two of the giant rubber and tyre manufacturers merged in 1970 to form the third largest tyre group in the world. Negotiation became difficult because Dunlop withdrew from the Joint Industrial Council in the UK and centralized its decision-making, while refusing to recognize the Shop Stewards' Combine Committee. After much fruitless pressure from the international trade union organizations, the shop stewards in Southampton made contact with the shop stewards in Milan. A simultaneous one-day stoppage at both these centres of production brought immediate recognition and established the beginnings of a long-term strategy of joint action by the British and Italian combine committees. This strategy went far beyond the joint preparation of wage demands to embrace jointly negotiated plans for new corporate investment. Proposals made originally by the merged company for cutting back employment were replaced by investment decisions that were designed to create new job opportunities.

The strength of the trade union action in Dunlop and Pirelli has rested on the direct contacts of the British and Italian shop stewards.

MICHELIN

Problems similar to those at Dunlop-Pirelli were faced by trade unions in the giant Michelin tyre company. In this case international cooperation was established at the top. Through the good offices of the International Federation of Chemical Workers, a Michelin World Trade Union Council was formed in June 1971 with delegates from France, Italy, Germany, Eire, Switzerland, Canada, Denmark, Algeria and Argentina. Their problem is that Michelin's worldwide activities are controlled from Basle in Switzerland. This enables the company to benefit from the low rates of company taxation in Switzerland and from the very limited disclosure of information required of companies under Swiss laws. It also creates special problems because Michelin has a major stake in both the Citroën and Fiat car companies in addition to its tyre manufacturing interests. Moreover, its joint activities with the American tyre company, Goodyear, are based on another tax haven, the island of Bermuda. The aims of the Michelin World Trade Union Council were drawn up to meet some of these problems by action under the following headings:

To co-ordinate collective bargaining and strikes;

To further the best conditions of employment prevailing in Michelin;

To collect and publish regular information bulletins;

To demand the right of decision in company investment plans;

To encourage and support the drive for union membership and organization at all Michelin plants.

The Council can show some successes in realizing these aims, but Charles Levinson, who describes them in his book *International Trade Unionism* (Allen & Unwin, 1972) was cautiously modest about progress up to that time.

INTERNATIONAL TRADE UNION COUNCILS FOR INDUSTRIES AND COMPANIES

The Michelin World Council is only one example of many world councils set up by international trade union organizations for specific industries and for trans-national companies.

The International Metalworkers Federation has created eight specific World Auto Councils, for General Motors, Ford, Chrysler, Volkswagen, Daimler-Benz, Fiat-Citroën, British Leyland and Renault-Peugeot, and it has recently established a Toyota-Nissan Council for South-East Asia. The first success of these councils was during the 1971 strike at Ford in Britain, when stewards and committee men from Dagenham met with their opposite numbers in Cologne and were given a pledge that Cologne workers would refuse to work overtime on material or parts normally made in the Dagenham or Halewood plants in Britain which were on strike. Other successes have included several moves towards the harmonization of working conditions.

We have tended in this chapter to concentrate on manufacturing firms, but the same process of increasing trans-national operations takes place in banking, insurance and retailing. The International Federation of Commercial, Clerical and Technical Employees has already begun to develop common action.

Action by trade unions in their relations with trans-national companies may be taken by combine committees, by national trade union centres, by international trade union organizations or by a combination of all three, which is what Levinson recommends. Trade union action may at the same time be directed primarily at the company concerned or less directly at governments and inter-governmental agencies. The actions taken by these means may be considered under three headings:

1. Obtaining and circulating information about trans-national companies' activities;
2. Exercising controls over their operating decisions and future policies;
3. Establishing international solidarity between workers in different countries.

With these means at their disposal the European Metalworkers' Federation, in association with the International Confederation of Trade Unions and the European TUC, laid down an action programme* in 1974 with the following six short-term goals:

1. Equality in status and equality of opportunity for migrant workers in Europe (most car workers in Europe are guest workers from southern Europe);
2. Greater influence for worker representatives on institutions of the European Economic Community;
3. Contacts and negotiations with European employer organizations in the metal industry;
4. Stronger direct action about the multinational corporations in Europe;
5. Coordination of national trade union policy of common interest;
6. Development of metalworkers' unions' joint goals and demands in future negotiations.

Since then ASTMS has established international committees bringing together unions from many different countries which have members working in Unilever, in Shell, in ICI and in CIBA-Geigy. You should find out what international contacts your union has with its opposite numbers in other countries which may be concerned with your industry and your company.

Once again, the information you have at the level of your involvement can only be effectively used in relation to information from other parts of a large organization and as part of an overall union policy for the organization.

*This programme is examined in detail in the author's essay, 'Working Class Internationalism and the Trans-national Company' in the resource book (published by Arrow Books) which accompanies this book, *Industrial Studies 3: understanding industrial society*. In particular the essay explores the work of the many institutions of the EEC in which European trade unions are now represented.

10. Carrying Out a Social Audit: Private Accounts and Social Costs

The Social Costs of Private Business

The closing down of plants in Britain, the transfer of investment overseas and the loss of jobs in mass redundancies may not be the worst problems facing British workers. The national press in the spring of 1976 recorded protests in several Lancashire towns about the levels of asbestos dust coming from local plants of the Turner and Newall group of companies, and the number of deaths of workers in recent years as a result of asbestosis. Early in 1972 there had been a similar outcry at the high concentrations of toxic metals building up in the Severn estuary, which were attributed to Rio Tinto Zinc's lead and zinc smelter at Avonmouth. The *Guardian* reported (28 January 1972): 'In the last eighteen months there have been at least 20 cases of serious lead poisoning at the factory. One hundred workers were at one time suspended from duty because of the lead level in their blood.' The *Observer* newspaper stated (30 January 1972) that 'Duncan Dewdney (the Chief Executive of RTZ in Britain) has openly confessed that the plant's initial construction was skimped, that corners were cut and that it should have cost at least two million pounds more'.

This is the heart of the matter. Health and safety, smoke abatement, air pollution control, the treatment of effluent, all cost money. In a competitive world companies seek to cut costs and we are all of us on the look-out for a cheaper product. So the Health and Safety Act lays duties on employers to ensure the health, safety and welfare of their employees, but qualifies this at every stage by adding the phrase 'so far as is reasonably practicable'.

WHAT IS REASONABLY PRACTICABLE?

The Alkali Inspectorate, according to *Social Audit* (vol. 2, no. 2, autumn 1974), is satisfied that the ICI dye works at Huddersfield are using the 'best practicable means' to dispose of oleum, sulphates and nitric acid when the top of its 200-foot chimney is just about on a level with the surrounding farmland. The CBI in a special report prepared in 1973, *The Responsibilities of the Public British Company*, speaks of keeping the 'right balance . . . between what is desirable and what can be afforded'.

The auditors of company accounts have to certify that the accounts give 'a true and fair view of the state of affairs' on a certain date of the profit, source and application of funds during the preceding year and that they comply with the Companies Act. They are not concerned with the human costs to the workers or the social costs to the community.

'It is the duty of Parliament', said the CBI Report, 'to ensure, as far as possible, that the operations of companies do not conflict with the public interest. . . .' The duties of the company are to 'behave like a good citizen in business'.

The CBI begins its Report by 'reiterating (its) belief in the private enterprise system and in the profit motive that sustains it. No other form of economic organization has demonstrated its ability to combine so great a capacity for satisfying the needs of society with provision for the individual of so large a measure of personal freedom. The mainspring of the private enterprise system is striving for profit.' But the Report recommends 'an imaginative concern for the well-being of the community from which the company derives its wealth'.

What Does the Law Say?

To master all the laws which regulate the operations of individual and commercial concerns today would be a mammoth task. But it is well worth knowing what Acts of Parliament do exist and what they cover:

The *Companies Acts* (the latest one is 1967), which we have already met, lay down what financial and other information must be disclosed to shareholders;

The *Factory Acts* and *Mines and Quarries Acts*, all comprehended in the *Health and Safety Act* of 1974, lay down the duties of employers and of employees and the rights of workers' representatives in all matters of health and safety;

The *Location of Industry Acts* and building licence regulations limit the rights of companies to build and operate where they choose;

The *Sanitary and Clean Air Acts* and local authority regulations require certain standards in relation to pollution of the environment;

The *Terms and Conditions of Employment Act* and *Wages Councils Acts* lay down minimum standards of pay and employment for workers not covered by trade union collective bargaining;

The *Trade Descriptions Act* controls the claims that can be made in marketing and advertising products;

The *Monopolies and Restrictive Practices Act* and the *Fair Trading Act* seek to limit the monopolistic position companies may take through mergers and takeovers;

The *Redundancy Payments Act* and *Industrial Training Act* both require companies to pay into common funds respectively for redundancy and for training and lay down the terms on which claims can be made on these funds;

The *Race Relations Act* and *Community Relations Act*, the *Sex Discrimination Act* and *Equal Pay Act* seek to prevent discrimination in employment and pay;

The *Employment Protection Act* guarantees the right of trade union membership and the recognition of and facilities for trade union representatives, and also provides against unfair dismissal and for paid maternity leave;

The *Trade Union and Labour Relations Act* legalizes the closed shop with some qualifications and gives certain limited rights of picketing;

The *Industry Act* of 1975 gives the Secretary of State the power to take companies into public ownership and to obtain information for the purpose of drawing up planning agreements with companies.

As well as all these Acts there are the Annual *Finance Acts* laying down rates and forms of corporate taxation; there are, too, exchange controls, import and export regulations and the codes laid down by the current incomes policy and by the Price Commission.

Information about Social Costs

Some of this legislation is described in Paul O'Higgins's book in this series called *Workers' Rights*, and other powers of government are described in another book in the series, Ann Taylor's *Trade Unions and Government*. What you need to consider here is the information you will require in order to check whether your company is acting in a socially responsible manner. The CBI Report quoted earlier ended with a list called 'Points of Public Interest'. These included points about pollution and environmental damage, conservation of materials and recycling, co-operation with local authorities and participation in community affairs and a whole number of points under the heading of 'National and International Affairs', such as imports from less developed countries, regard for minority groups, career guidance. The fact is, however, that companies are in business to make money. Even government legislation only applies 'as far as is reasonably practical' and within the 'striving for profit' advocated by the CBI. Nevertheless, it is clear that many firms are increasingly worried about the social costs of business enterprise. The image of untrammelled free enterprise has become distinctly tarnished and the costs of sickness, waste and extravagance are real. There is even money to be made now, as well as heavy costs to the state, in palliating what should never have been committed in the first place.

This situation offers great opportunities for the active trade unionist. Questions about social cost involve revelations of things that some managements would rather keep quiet about.

Knowledge Gives Power

Access to information gives power. Most industrial democracy consists of the democratizing of knowledge. The organizations which will help you to find the information you need are reviewed in the last part of this book (pp. 105–27). Before calling them in, you must decide what you want to know. There is only space here to look briefly at three areas: health and safety; current industrial strategy and longer-term planning agreements. Then we shall consider the possible extension of the idea of a social audit.

HEALTH AND SAFETY

The key questions here are:

1. What is the product or what are the products you are working with? What hazards are associated with them, with the materials going into them or coming from them or with the processes of production?

2. What are the maximum safe levels of exposure for workers and the surrounding community and environment? Remember this may mean levels affecting the ears, lungs and blood of those

inside and outside the plant, as well as the more direct physical dangers of handling and the more obvious pollution of air, land and water.

3. What tests are made and at what intervals and what access do unions have to the results?

4. What accident records are kept and how are they analysed and what access do unions have to the results?

5. What opportunities exist for trade union representatives to be involved in health and safety committees, to make their own independent inspections, to be present at Inspectors' visits, to stop work in the event of accidents, to take part in the planning

Carbonization plant, East Midlands. Photo: Henry Grant

of premises and design of plant to make them as safe and healthy as possible, and to be trained for these duties?

INDUSTRIAL STRATEGY

In 1976 the unions were restricted by the Labour Government's pay policy, Stage II, to a rise in pay up to August 1977 of 5 per cent with a cash minimum of £2·50 and a maximum of £4 a week. This followed Stage I of the pay policy which set a limit for the year of £6 above previous rates. At the same time, by contrast, the limits on employers' price increases were steadily relaxed, with the aim of encouraging companies, particularly in manufacturing industry, to use the higher profit margins allowed to step up their capital investment. The object was to make British industry more competitive and able therefore to employ more people and correct the unfavourable balance of imports and exports in foreign trade. We looked in the last chapter at some of the problems of foreign trade caused by the policies of the trans-national companies. The key question for trade unionists in considering the Labour Government's industrial strategy is whether companies will in fact take advantage of the higher prices they can charge and of their subsequent higher profits, to invest in new plant to increase employment opportunities in Britain, or whether they will rather invest abroad or in commodities or property speculation. Trade unionists need to monitor the social benefits of such policies very carefully.

Here is an excerpt from 'Industrial Strategy: A Checklist for Trade Union Representatives', a paper drawn up by the TUC in its *Economic Review for 1976* which had to take into account the stagnation and actual fall of industrial output between 1974 and 1976. Every active trade unionist was encouraged to have a copy (free from your union or from the TUC, Congress House, Great Russell Street, London WC1), and to require management to go through it and provide answers for each question. The dates can be changed but the questions remain relevant.

Economic Background

89. ... (i) What are the plans of your company for output in the coming three years?

(ii) Are sectors and companies confident that they will be able to meet both the upturn in world trade and increased demand at home?

Investment

90. (i) What are the investment plans of companies and sectors in the coming five-year period?

(ii) What is the scope for bringing forward investment programmes into 1976 to prepare for increased demand in 1977?

(iii) Has the company considered applying for selective assistance under the Industry Act scheme? Is the company aware of the September closing date for application for the accelerated capital projects scheme?

(iv) Union representatives should press companies to set maximum levels of investment taking place abroad; are companies satisfied that investment would not be more worthwhile in the UK?

(v) What is the age of capital equipment in companies? Union representatives should press for an inventory in each company; sector working parties should collect information for the sector; where the average age of plant and machinery is above that of the most efficient 20 per cent of firms, there is a *prima facie* case for new investment.

New Markets and Products

91. (i) What are the prospects for finding new export markets?

(ii) What new products can be developed?

(iii) Has the company taken full advantage of the British Overseas Trade Board's services?

(iv) Has the company involved trade union representatives in trade missions overseas?

Bottlenecks

92. (i) Does the company or sector make a product which is liable to be in short supply in the upturn? What are the prospects for building up stocks in 1976?

(ii) Is the company satisfied that it will not itself be short of materials or components because of bottlenecks in the upturn?

(iii) What action can be taken in 1976 to relieve potential bottlenecks?

Manpower

93. (i) What are the manpower plans in each sector or company?

(ii) If a company is considering redundancies has it considered the cost of disbanding a skilled workforce?

(iii) Is the company willing to apply for the Temporary Employment Subsidy?

(iv) What steps is the company taking to increase training, particularly of young people?

(v) What scope is there for encouraging short-time working as an alternative to redundancies?

Imports

94. . . . Import penetration has been defined as the percentage share of imports in total sales on the domestic market. The latter total is calculated by subtracting exports from estimated gross sales and adding in imports. . . .

(i) Generally speaking there should be no further increase in import penetration above present levels and in certain sectors strong efforts should be made to reduce the import penetration figure. The import penetration ceiling figures should be agreed as a matter of urgency. Will companies and sectors set import penetration ceilings for the next three years?

(ii) Will companies consider measures needed to promote import substitution and the impact on domestic output?

(iii) Will companies review purchases from abroad and the extent to which requirements could be met from UK resources?

(iv) Unions in the distribution sector should press for full information on purchases from abroad. Can distributors buy more British goods?

PLANNING AGREEMENTS

If your company has reached a planning agreement with the Government, then the unions have the right to be involved and you should be able to obtain a copy and consider what implications it has for your work and how you can best monitor the way that it is being carried out. But you will probably have to fight for your rights. The general objectives of these agreements have been indicated by the Government in the Industry Act as follows in the list below with the general aims of encouraging companies 'to align their plans with national needs'.

Where these objectives are being fulfilled, Government loans and grants may be made available:

1. To promote employment by investment in assisted areas and to underwrite certain levels of regional assistance;
2. To conserve resources, including energy in both the productive processes and products concerned;
3. To overcome 'inadequacies in the supply of particular materials and components that may cause bottlenecks for other sections of industry';
4. To expand exports as a share of production, to minimize imports and to develop import substitutes;

5. To improve industrial productivity and company performance in key sectors of industry;
6. To consider the interests of the community, for instance, equal opportunity and other employment policies; noise levels and effluent disposal.

In the Government's discussion document issued by the Department of Industry in 1975, 'The Contents of a Planning Agreement', from which these objectives are taken, reference is made to the need for 'workers to be consulted about and involved in companies' forward plans' and to 'plans being drawn up by management in close consultation with trade union representatives from the firm'.

In order to give trade union work-place representatives an idea of what might be involved in a planning agreement, ASTMS drew up a first draft of one in 1975 as part of a union discussion document, 'The Crisis of British Economic Planning'. You should write to the head office of ASTMS (10–26 Jamestown Road, London NW1) for a copy, since it provides a basic model for trade unionists to refer to.

What is a Social Audit?

So far we have looked at the private accounts and social costs of individual companies; but these do not operate in isolation from the wider community. The larger the company, the greater its impact on society. The loss of 25000 jobs at Chrysler would certainly have led to unemployment for a further 25000 workers in companies supplying Chrysler and maybe considerably more, as reduced purchases by these 50000 would affect employment elsewhere. Where such large-scale effects are likely, proposals have been made for a social audit.

The idea of a social audit as something distinct from the auditing of a company's accounts goes back to studies of the social costs of private enterprise in the 1950s and the more recent need to make estimates of social costs and benefits, when big public investments in schemes like the Channel Tunnel or a new London airport or the Victoria underground line were being considered. Private calculations of the likely yield on capital invested do not provide the information required to determine the costs and benefits to the public of such schemes, especially when large

Government subsidies are involved and a major change in the environment will result. But more and more schemes come into this category today as the scale of the investment and the implications for the environment grow. When the closure of the Upper Clyde Shipbuilders in 1971 was being challenged by the workers, and later when Imperial Typewriters closed their British factories in 1975, a demand was made for a social audit which would take into account the costs of social security and also of the other social costs of closing down economic activities in areas where levels of unemployment were already high.

At the time of the threatened closure of Upper Clyde Shipbuilders, and of the closure of Imperial Typewriters' plants in Hull and Leicester, calculations were made which showed a potential cost over two years of £15m on the Clydeside and £2m in Hull on social security provisions alone, and many times these figures in capital costs of providing new employment, housing and other services elsewhere. These sums could be compared with the £6m and £3m respectively for UCS and Imperial which were needed to restart production. Of course, this is not to say that all current economic activities should always be continued and that no workers should ever be made redundant in one employment and thus available for other work. What it does mean is that such changes could be planned for, and made subject to a process of social audit which would supplement and complement the private accounting of enterprises and companies. In this way resources could be allocated to best advantage through democratic procedures of consultation, and waste and unemployment could thus be avoided.

This was one of the main purposes in the proposal for planning agreements, according to one of the people most involved in shaping the Labour Party's commitment to such planning measures in its 1974 Manifestos.

> The Social Audit of the published Planning Agreements would in itself vastly democratise the process of strategic decision-making in the economy. When the government has decided to impose particular features of a Planning Agreement on an enterprise, it could publish the reasons for its decision in the Social Audit. The Audit could particularly stress the consumer implications of the enterprise's activity, including the past overall record on consumer pricing, terms of sale, advertising expenditure, identified as a proportion of the cost of itemised household products, deterioration or improvement in the

quality of public service, misleading or deceptive advertising, success or failure in meeting complaints on imperfect goods and services, and so on. (From Stuart Holland, *Strategy for Socialism*, Spokesman Books, 1975, p. 67.)

The private sector, the public sector of nationalized corporations and central and local government are all equally involved in such a social audit. Each depends on the other; and, while the private sector is taxed to finance public services, it is generally the case that it is heavily dependent on subsidies from the public sector. The Dunlop Rubber Company has frankly admitted that it made a profit from regional aid which was useful for investment elsewhere. At the same time gas competes against electricity, road against rail, sea against air. The results can be both costly and socially wasteful.

Some shop stewards in big companies in large industrial areas have already begun to think about establishing social funds for local community needs into which their taxes might be paid under new forms of local income tax; and the Lucas Aerospace stewards have drawn up a corporate plan for new lines of production which would replace the declining market for aircraft. These are just the beginning of what could become a major concern of trade unionists.

The combination of social audit and planning agreements could provide the basis for a much wider process of planning. At the Committee of Inquiry into the closure of UCS in 1971 the proposal was made that:

a Social Audit to establish the case for public investment in UCS would have to go beyond the direct accounts of the company, and even beyond the direct costs and benefits of its continued operation as a public concern. It would have in effect to open up an inquiry into the full use of the human and natural resources of Scotland. What is required is a Scottish economic plan for full employment. The resources of universities, technical colleges and all industrial and trade union research departments should be called upon immediately to provide staff:

first, for making an inventory

(a) of the urgent social needs of the people,

(b) of economic resources including man power, education and training facilities and plant and equipment existing in Scotland,

(c) of resources needed from outside Scotland and Scotland's capacity to pay them;

and *secondly*, for drawing up an emergency economic plan leading on to a longer term plan for economic development.

Funds would have to be made available immediately for teams to get down to this work and for local authorities, trade unions and other voluntary bodies to take part in what would become a national audit.

Scotland has a special interest in such a study, but Wales and the regions of England too have similar interests. Closure by BSC of its Hartlepool works was being proposed in 1976, at a time when the North of England Regional Development Council was predicting 26 per cent unemployment in the town and 20 per cent in the region. What trade union activists can do is to stimulate their company managements and local authorities into setting up local social audit groups. All past experience suggests that social costs cannot be left to companies or to Government legislation to audit and to control. Trade union committees in major companies, corporations and public bodies are already combining with neighbourhood action groups and specialized pressure groups to tackle urgent problems affecting the environment in many areas. An example is the North East Trade Union Studies Unit supported by some Tyneside trade unions and combine committees. The test of its success, according to its first report, depended upon its capacity to make available a reliable and practical research service to its constituent members.

The rest of this book is designed to help the trade union activist to develop his own research and information service. But it will be constantly emphasized that this will always be more effective when it is done in conjunction with official union bodies and associated organizations which already have a wide range of services at their members' disposal. The TUC in its 1976 *Economic Review* expressed concern at the delay in implementing the proposal for planning agreements made in the 1975 Industry Act, and recommended a positive campaign to encourage firms to enter into them (since the Industry Act had been shorn of compulsory powers) and the offer of formal incentives by way of special Government help for investment. There is all the more reason why trade unionists should take their own steps through combine committees, trades councils, local authorities and regional development councils to involve employers and Government in the type of action proposed for Scotland at the time of the threatened closure of UCS.

In these big questions of social accounting you will need to work together with other unions, Trades Councils and regional organizations and academics in preparing plans and strategies of common interest to all workers.

St Michael News

MARKS & SPENCER JUNE 1976

SPECIAL REPORT

HOW WE ARE DOING

The fast selling St Michael £2.50 nylon polo neck was, as The Sunday Times reported, "the highest selling woman's garment of all in Britain in 1975."

M & S is one of Britain's largest retail chains. We sell the most clothes and are the fifth largest seller of food. We have just announced our sales and profits for the last twelve months.

This year, for the first time, the figures include our companies in Canada and Europe as well as our UK stores and exports.

This special report to staff on how the business is doing uses the successful £2.50 polo neck to illustrate

* how we pay our way
* how we help to earn the nation's daily bread
* and how inflation has caused us all a lot of headaches over the past year.

We earn our living in M & S by selling things. We do it on a huge scale. Last year, about 1,500,000,000 sales were rung up, bringing in a total of £949,000,000.

What happens to all that money? For the answer, let us look at what happens to each £2.50 spent by our customers on for example polo neck sweaters.

The picture (right) shows how the money is divided up. The share-out applies to the total £949 million of sales.

What happens is that out of each £2.50 that goes into the till, £1.97 goes straight back out of the business to pay suppliers for stock, to meet running costs like rates, heat and light and to pay VAT to the Government.

The 53p that is left has to pay salaries, tax to the Government, dividends to shareholders, and provide for future growth.

The biggest and most important thing we pay for out of this 53p is staff pay, pension scheme contributions, national insurance, amenities, welfare facilities and other benefits.

When we've paid for these essential costs, we are left with 27p. That is our 'before tax profit'.

The Government takes away over half of it, leaving us with 13p. This has to be split two ways.

About 6½p is to pay dividends to shareholders who have put their money into the business to help it grow. And like our pay, there are strict Government limits on how much we can pay out.

We keep the last 6½p inside the business. Most is spent on building new stores and improving those we already have so that we can sell more and expand. This is investment. And some is saved to spend on replacing store equipment and furniture when it wears out. This is what we set aside for depreciation.

This sweater sells at £2.50. What happens to the money?

STOCK & EXPENSES

£1.97

Most of the money put in the till buys stock and pays expenses like rates, heat, light, phones. And 18p is VAT which goes straight to the Government.

What happens to the 53p that is left?

FOR STAFF **26p**

Pays salaries, national insurance, bonuses, pensions, amenities and welfare.

TAX ON PROFIT **14p**

Government takes over half of what is left after staff costs have been paid.

INVESTMENT **6½p**

Pays for new stores and replaces old and out of date equipment.

DIVIDENDS **6½p**

Distributed among 250,000 shareholders who have invested their money in the business.

Part III: How to Collect and Analyse the Information

11. Reading Company Reports

Companies nowadays publish a great deal of information about themselves. But you may need to look for more than one document. You will find:

1. The Report to the Employees, if there is one;
2. The Chairman's Statement to the Shareholders;
3. The Report to the Shareholders;
4. The Accounts.

The last two are generally published together to give all the information required under the Companies Act; the first two may be issued separately.

The Report to the Employees

You might as well start with the Report to the Employees, since it is meant for you and is generally in simpler language than the Report to the Shareholders, with photographs of the chairman and coloured charts and graphs. It is sometimes called the 'Mug's Guide' by people who are experts at accounts; but if you discount the propaganda line about our great company all pulling together as one team, there is much to be learned from it as an introduction to the full Report to the Shareholders.

The most valuable information here, which is often not supplied in the Shareholders' Report, is the breakdown of costs and sales to show the cost of materials and services bought in. From this, as we saw in Chapter 5, we can deduce the value added. You must remember that the proportion of sales value that is made up of bought-in items will vary enormously amongst companies in different lines of business. A store like Marks and Spencer reveals that the cost of a sweater selling at £2·50 will be made up to the extent of nearly £2 (80 per cent) of bought-in stock, light, heat, VAT and other items paid out. By contrast, the cost of bought-in

items accounts for only about 60 per cent of the value of ICI's sales. This is why we saw that the ratio of profit to value added is so much more important than the ratio of profit to turnover.

Other points of interest you may find in the Report to Employees will concern research and development, health and safety, social costs and concern for the environment and other matters that directors are becoming sensitive about these days.

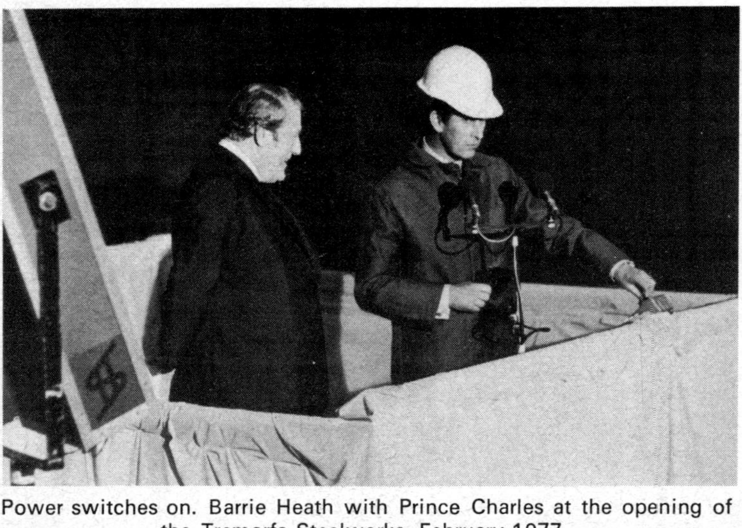

Power switches on. Barrie Heath with Prince Charles at the opening of the Tremorfa Steelworks, February 1977

The Chairman's Statement

The next publication you should look for is the Chairman's Statement to the Shareholders. This may or may not be at the beginning of the Report and Accounts, but should be read first.

It will contain a summary of the most important points in the Report with some words of explanation, and, most important, some indication of future prospects. This is the only part of the Report that will give you a laugh, so enjoy it while you can. Chairmen love to pontificate about world events and tend to have a positively schoolmasterish attitude to the good old school (company). One of these is Barrie Heath, chairman of GKN.

By 1975 many chairmen were writing about the need for worker participation. As Barrie Heath said: 'Industrial democracy is a new catch-phrase for a developing process of enlightened management that has been the policy of GKN over many years.' This is an important statement for all stewards.

Don't miss the nuggets of real information about future plans like Barrie Heath's announcement in his 1975 Report that GKN was buying a 75 per cent interest in the West German clutch and shock absorber manufacturers, the Sachs Group, with 16000 employees, for 330m Deutschmarks.

The Report to the Shareholders

This will be divided up into several parts with information tucked away in many corners. You should look for the following:

THE DIRECTORS AND SHAREHOLDERS AND ASSOCIATED COMPANIES

The names of the chairman, vice-chairman and board of directors will be listed at the beginning of the Report. You can find what other boards they sit on by looking them up in the *Directory of Directors* in your local library. If you want to know more about them and their family connections, you may find them in *Who's Who* or in Debrett's *Peerage* (if they are in the House of Lords), and also in your library. Some firms are family firms and some are owned by financial groups. You will find these listed in K. Coates (ed.), *Can the Workers Run Industry?* (Sphere Books,

1968), Chapter 2, 'Who Controls British Industry?' Many of the other companies your directors direct will be subsidiaries or associated companies; and these must be listed somewhere in the Report of the parent company, together with details of the share held by the parent company in their capital. The directors must state in the Report what holdings of the company's shares they have, or their families have, and they must reveal the chairman's pay and the number of directors at different rates of remuneration (pay and emoluments) and the pay of employees earning over £10000 a year. An analysis of shareholders by size of holding and breakdown between individuals and institutions also has to be included. If you want more details you will have to go to the Companies' Registry at Cardiff, or ask the Labour Research Department to search for you. (If your union is not a subscriber to LRD, you can subscribe for less than £5 a year.)

THE YEAR IN BRIEF: SALIENT FIGURES AND GROUP FINANCIAL RECORD

After studying the Chairman's Statement and lists of directors and companies, look for a summary of the Report under some such title as the above. The Record will enable you to see the figures in the current Report and Accounts in relation to what has gone before. There should be a ten-year or five-year run of figures giving the financial record of assets, capital, sales and profits. Some of the key ratios may have been worked out for you. Look out, for example, for:

1. The dividend per share (in pence);
2. The earnings per share (in pence). Earnings will be after providing for depreciation, taxation and loan interest;
3. The ratio of earnings to EQUITY INTEREST (per cent). Note that equity interest equals the issued share capital plus reserves (that is, the claims of ordinary shareholders excluding claims on the company from any medium- or long-term borrowing).

In large companies you may have to distinguish the group accounts, for which summaries and record are provided, and the parent company accounts, which may be shown separately in the Accounts or in the Notes to the Accounts. The group accounts will also show any outside shareholders' interests.

There are three other points to look for:

1. Changes in gearing: ordinary capital compared to other sources of finance;
2. Changes in taxation paid, *less* grants received;
3. Changes in depreciation provision. There may be a table giving figures for earnings after depreciation and for capital expenditure.

Here are the figures for the GKN Group:

Table 24: The Source and Use of Funds, GKN Group, 1971–5 (£m)

	1971	*1972*	*1973*	*1974*	*1975*
Depreciation provision	19·96	23·55	26·33	34·04	41·89
Earnings after depreciation (and after tax outside interest)	21·67	26·65	28·27	38·06	20·07
Total above funds	41·63	50·20	54·60	72·10	61·96
Capital expenditure	27·74	18·22	28·30	50·70	63·64

This is of course a very incomplete table of sources and use of funds. In some years there were other sources of funds, such as increases in stocks, purchases of and investments in other companies. But the greater part of the difference in amount between the last two lines in the first few years of the table will be explained by payments of dividends and by additions to reserves. You need to watch these over a run of several years because the aim of building up reserves is to expand the business; and employees need to know how these reserves are going to be used just as much as the shareholders do. You might look especially for a figure of capital expenditure 'sanctioned but not spent'.

THE REPORT OF THE DIRECTORS

The heart of the Company Report is the Report of the Directors and you should read this next. In the case of public corporations, the Report follows straight on from the Chairman's Statement and there may, in addition, be a separate set of statistical tables.

The Coal Board, for example, publishes these separately now. It should include:

1. A review of trading operations with details of sales turnover and profits by area and by product with details of exports (profits on exports may be shown separately), new contracts, use of capacity, price movements;
2. The results of associated companies;
3. A report on the assets employed, any revaluation of assets that has taken place, additions to assets and depreciation provision;
4. A review of the sources of finance, new share capital and other borrowings;
5. A statement of the total number of employees and total remuneration (this is the minimum the law requires and is quite useless for bargaining purposes without further breakdown);
6. The recommendation of the dividend to be paid per share for the Annual General Meeting of the shareholders to authorize;
7. A statement required by law of any donations to political parties, charities, etc.;
8. Reports of the death or pending retirement of the chairman and directors and nominations for their replacement by vote of the shareholders – a farce this, as no one nominated by the board is ever opposed except in a crisis situation.

The Accounts

These will be at the back of the Report. They will be preceded or followed by some important notes.

ACCOUNTING POLICIES

This is the 'small print' that really matters in the Accounts. You cannot read them through like a novel, but this is what you should look for:

1. What rates of depreciation are used and what additional depreciation is added for inflation;
2. How stocks are valued and at what date they were valued;
3. How taxation is applied, particularly deferred taxation;

Notes to the Accounts

ACCOUNTING POLICIES

The accounting policies of the Group are explained, as applicable, under the appropriate headings in the Notes to the Accounts, subject to the following:—

(a) The accounts of the Company and of its subsidiaries are made up to 31st March.

(b) Profit from Group Trading includes profit on inter-Group Sales made in the ordinary course of business. Turnover, including inter-Group Sales, is given in paragraph 2 of the Directors' Report.

(c) The trading results, assets and liabilities of overseas subsidiaries, branches and associated companies are expressed in sterling at the rates ruling on 31st March.

(d) Associated Companies (the principal ones are listed on page 17) are investments in which the Company has a beneficial interest of at least 20 per cent in the equity share capital and the Company has special rights of representation on the boards of directors.

1 SALES

Comprise sales to customers outside the Group and are after elimination of all inter-Group transactions. In the case of rental income the amounts charged to customers are included as sales. Long-term contracts are not invoiced until contracts are completed or part deliveries made.

2 PROFIT BEFORE TAXATION

	1976 £ million	1975 £ million
This comprises:—		
(a) Profit from Group Trading	183.6	141.2
(b) Share of Profits *less* Losses of Associated Companies	14.6	12.7
(c) Interest and Investment Income	9.0	11.3
	207.2	165.2

4. How group accounts have been consolidated from the different company accounts;

5. How foreign exchange transactions have been calculated.

NOTES TO THE ACCOUNTS

These are the most important:

1. The details of stocks that may distinguish between raw materials and finished products;

2. The details of taxation paid and grants received (if these are distinguished) and of tax relief on stock appreciation;

3. The details of fixed assets: disposals, additions and depreciation for separate items, land, buildings, plant, machinery, vehicles, work in progress;

4. The details of capital structure, medium- and long-term borrowing, secured and unsecured debentures, repayment dates and rates of interest paid;

5. Trade investments and credits to contractors. These may be distinguished from relations with associated companies and should be watched to reveal the way funds are being used outside the company;

6. Comparisons between the group and the parent company's credits and debits in the current assets may reveal another way that funds are being used. Here is an example from ICI:

Table 25: ICI Group and Company Debtors and Creditors 1973, 1974, 1975 (£m)

	1973	*1974*	*1975*	*1975 balance*
ICI Group: debtors	569·5	667·4	711	+67
creditors	508·5	634·0	644	
ICI Company: debtors	34·4	53·4	51	−229
creditors	235·1	288·9	280	
ICI Group outside company: debtors	535·1	614·0	660	+296
creditors	273·4	345·1	364	

Note that the company appears to have been in effect borrowing from the rest of the group in each year to the extent of £200m or more. This was presumably because the company was responsible for the greater part of new investment – fine if you work for the company, not so good if you work for one of the companies taken into the group.

THE ACCOUNTS THEMSELVES

This leaves only the Accounts themselves for you to study. They will be set out as we have seen earlier.

1. A *profit and loss account* for the year and previous year indicating what profit is applicable to the company (the parent company in group accounts) and what changes have been made in reserves.

2. *Balance sheets* at the end of the year and previous year indicating assets employed and how they are financed (for group and company in group accounts).

3. The *source and application of funds* for the year and previous year. This table may be included in the Report and not in the Accounts (and in group accounts will be shown only for the group as a whole).

INFLATION-ADJUSTED ACCOUNTS

At the end of the Accounts there will be a statement of the effect of adjusting the group or company accounts by expressing all the amounts in terms of the purchasing power of the £ at the end of the accounting period on the so-called current purchasing power (CPP) or current cost accounting (CCA) basis instead of the conventional historic cost. These accounting systems were referred to in Chapter 5. You will need help from a tutor or an accountant if you want to understand them.

THE AUDITOR'S REPORT

This often contains an important statement of reservations. Auditors are independent accountants who have to apply standard accounting practice to the accounts they audit. They may ask for extra information and two firms of auditors may honestly and respectably disagree. In the case of the bid in 1969 by the American controlled Leasco World Trading Co. (UK) Ltd for Robert Maxwell's Pergamon Press Ltd, the disagreement amounted to many millions of £s in the values set upon the stock of unsold books. So beware, and watch the small print. And remember the chairman's statement is *not* subject to audit.

Finally, you will need to use the information in the Report in relation to the other information you have for your part of the company and in relation to the policy your union organization is pursuing. The Annual Report is made to the shareholders. To turn it to your ends you must use it for the clues it gives you to the other information you need to obtain.

12. Drawing upon Official Information

About fifteen years ago a Conservative Prime Minister, Harold Macmillan, compared the economic decisions he had to make on the basis of Government statistics with the dilemma of a man making a railway journey across Britain on the basis of last year's *Bradshaw*. No one had told Macmillan that Bradshaw's had ceased to publish a comprehensive railway timetable (there was no longer a comprehensive railway service); but the point was a good one. Since then the available statistics have become much more up-to-date and much more extensive. There are still long delays between the taking of and the publication of a major census – like the five-year General Household Census and the Census of Production. Annual statistics tend to relate to a year that ended more than a year before the date of publication. However, monthly and quarterly series of publications covering a wide range of subjects now appear within a month or so of the events they describe. They provide the essential national statistics against which to compare the performance of your own union, company or organization.

Sources You Can Consult

There are three or four (weekly or monthly) statistical journals issued by Government departments, which contain the main series of official statistics. They are listed below. Unless, however, you are a combine committee member or a full-time union officer you will probably not have the time or money to use these sources regularly. You will rely on what you can get hold of from your union, from the TUC, from WEA publications, from the Labour Research Department's *Fact Service* and *Labour Research*, and from the Ruskin College Trade Union Research Unit.

But the official publications will be in your local library and if you want to find answers to specific problems it is useful to know

CENTRAL STATISTICAL OFFICE
Trends
Department of Employment
Trade and Industry
14 January 1977 35p
CENTRAL STATISTICAL OFFICE
Trends
Department of Employment Gazette
Trade and Industry
January 1977 35p
British boatbuilders hoist their sales

where to look for them. What this chapter does, then, is first to list the main journals and then go through all the many problems for which you might want to find answers by studying the statistics. Obviously you won't want to tackle all or even many of the studies suggested here; you need only glance through this chapter, so that you will be able to find the right sources here for answering your problems.

The three main journals are the following (all published by HMSO, PO Box 569, London SE1):

Trade and Industry (weekly) carries selected indicators of the state of the economy each week and several of the key series of industrial output, home and foreign trade statistics. The index at the back will tell you when each series is published. This journal carries news and articles on different industries and an invaluable section giving answers by Ministers to questions in Parliament;

Economic Trends (monthly) carries the main series on the economy as a whole: national income and expenditure (private and public, current and capital), balance of payments, cyclical indicators, and regular articles on the incidence of taxes, input-output tables, company finance, etc.;

The Department of Employment *Gazette* (monthly) carries the key series on movements in wage rates and earnings, productivity, retail prices, employment, unemployment and unfilled vacancies. It also has articles on youth employment, health and safety, manpower projections, labour turnover, etc.

In addition to the journals there is a valuable digest called the *Monthly Digest of Statistics* which carries in summary form a bit of everything, including population, education, housing and social statistics, as well as the main series from the other journals and some regional statistics.

You will need to be able to refer to all four of the above if you are to follow national trends and relate them to your own local problems and experience. This will become clear if we look at the information needed for five major trade union functions:

1. National wage negotiation;
2. Company, plant and productivity bargaining;
3. Dealing with rationalization, redundancy and unemployment;
4. Monitoring international movements of goods and capital;

5. Carrying out a social audit of health and safety, investment intentions and economic plans.

Before trying to handle statistics in their raw form in the journals and digests, you should study another book in this series, Karl Hedderwick's *Statistics for Bargainers*.

National Wage Negotiation

You may want to know the level and movement of wages rates and earnings in all industries and in particular industries in order to compare with your own. For real wages you will need the retail price index and for real take-home pay the INCIDENCE of taxes and benefits on different types of household. And wage movements should be compared with movements in productivity and profits.

WAGES

Your starting point must be the *New Earnings Survey* carried out each year in April and published in the autumn in summary form in the Department of Employment *Gazette*. You can get the complete survey in six instalments. It is a must for all union negotiating teams. You can find wage levels broken down into their make-up: basic, PREMIUM, overtime, by manual and non-manual, male and female, full-time and part-time, by occupation and industry, Joint Industrial Councils and Wages Councils, with hours worked, earnings by length of service and numbers and proportions in each category and at each level.

In between surveys you will have to make use of:

1. The monthly index of manual workers' wage rates and hours;
2. The monthly index of all employees' earnings by industry;
3. The half-yearly hourly and weekly earnings figures for male manual workers in certain manufacturing industries.

All these are published in the Department of Employment *Gazette*.

PRICES

The retail price index is also published monthly in the *Gazette*, with detailed figures for different items for all households, with pensioner households separately. The way households with different levels of income spend it is shown in the annual *Household Expenditure Survey* which indicates how movements in the prices of different items will affect different households. Actual prices paid in retail shops and markets are also given monthly in the *Gazette* and wholesale prices appear annually in *Trade and Industry* with a monthly index in between.

PRODUCTIVITY

Movements in the index of output per person employed in different industries and of output per man hour in manufacturing appear monthly in the *Gazette*, and also in *Economic Trends*. Remember that in all these figures output is measured in real terms, after discounting for any price increases. Figures published of earnings per unit of output are therefore of money earnings (not real earnings) per units of output in real terms (not money terms). Productivity figures in the coal industry appear in the monthly (free) publication, *Energy Trends*, from the Department of Energy, Thames House (South), Millbank, London SW1.

PROFITS

Figures for all companies' profits appear in *Economic Trends* in the tables of 'Shares of Income' and 'Appropriation Accounts of Companies'. To find a breakdown by industry is more difficult. You have to get the *Financial Times Quoted Companies Record of the Year* published early in January. For individual companies from the top thousand you will find figures of profits and much other useful information derived from company accounts in *The Times 1000*, published annually by *The Times* newspaper (New Printing House Square, Gray's Inn Road, London WC1).

Company, Plant and Productivity Bargaining

To find national figures to compare with your own, you will have to go to the same sources for many of the items referred to above. For very large companies like ICI you can get the print-out of the *New Earnings Survey* covering the sample one per cent of employees surveyed. This will give you some valuable figures of the distribution of earnings, hours worked, proportion of overtime pay in total earnings, etc. You will need help in analysing it from your union research office or the Trade Union Research Unit, Ruskin College, Oxford.

To find value-added figures for each industry there is only the *Census of Production* and *Census of Distribution* to go to. These give net output (roughly the same as value added) for all firms and for large firms in each industry. For each census, there is a big five-yearly sample survey; and a smaller sample provides an *Annual Census of Production* reported in *Trade and Industry*. The state corporations (nationalized industries) publish figures from which you can deduce the value added; and it is high time all companies in the private sector did likewise. One useful set of figures is the monthly and quarterly estimates of stocks, broken down by industry, published in *Trade and Industry*.

Dealing with Rationalization, Redundancy and Unemployment

The main source of information here must be the figures of employment and unemployment and unfilled vacancies, male and female, by industry, region and occupation, with special figures for youth and immigrants. All these are in the Department of Employment *Gazette*. Unemployment rates and numbers are given for the groups of local employment offices and for the assisted areas. Sources of Government assistance for employment are regularly described in the *Gazette* and regional grants for investment are given monthly and quarterly in *Trade and Industry*. Quarterly capital expenditure figures by industry and region also appear in *Trade and Industry*, and so does news of ACQUISITIONS and mergers. What companies in general are doing with their money can be found in *Economic Trends* under the heading of 'Sources and Use of Funds'.

Estimates of future employment trends are given in a series, 'Cyclical Indicators for the UK Economy', also in *Economic Trends*. It will be your own employer's plans that are most important to you, and he will be in touch with the local employment exchange and Youth Employment Office and regional officials of the Department of Employment and Department of Industry; but it will be well worth your while to have your own contacts. The local Trades Council and the bigger unions will have representatives on local employment committees, and your political contacts, councillors and MPs, will have access to much official information.

Monitoring International Movements of Goods and Capital

If you work for a multinational company you will want to know about its exports and imports, its transfer pricing policies and its movements of capital from country to country. Since the big companies operating trans-nationally are responsible for between a third and a half of all Britain's trade, and individual companies may be responsible for much larger shares even than that in particular product lines, the total British trade figures should prove helpful. Overall figures for exports and imports by COMMODITY groups and areas are published quarterly in *Trade and Industry*. Capital movements and other items entering the balance of payments appear quarterly in *Economic Trends*.

For details of exports and imports by individual commodities and countries you will have to go to the *Overseas Trade Statistics* of the UK. These are published by HMSO monthly and the most useful issues are those for January and July which give totals for the previous year and six months respectively. Figures of quantities are given as well as values, so that you can work out average prices. These accounts provide the most complete picture of the actual movement of goods and prices that is available for any part of the British economy. Combined with your own inside information of your company's products, you should be able to piece together a clear idea of the contribution your company is making to the success or failure of Britain's trade balance. A valuable supplementary source of information in this field will be the trade journal of the manufacturers' association to which your company belongs. The *Motor Manufacturers' and Traders' Journal*, in particular, provides much information about exports, imports and prices.

There are no similarly detailed figures of capital movements. The surveys of direct company investment overseas and of direct exporters' credit terms made by the Department of Trade, and published annually in *Trade and Industry* (and in somewhat greater detail in the Department of Industry's *Business Monitor* series) are always at least two years out of date and give only the most general breakdown by industry and area. Nonetheless, combined with other information from company accounts and from answers to Parliamentary questions about Government credits, grants and loans for overseas business, at least some corners of the jigsaw puzzle can be pieced together successfully. This is the area where the planning agreements to be reached by Government and companies with trade union involvement could make their main contribution to the disclosure of much information that is now concealed, but should be public knowledge in a democratic society.

Carrying Out a Social Audit

Three headings (see pp. 94–9) were suggested for an audit of the wider social effects of your employment. The information now becoming available under each heading makes this a much more worthwhile exercise.

HEALTH AND SAFETY

The death and accident statistics published in the Department of Employment *Gazette* have never been very valuable because they only give totals for ill-defined industrial categories without relation to man-hours of work. The Annual Report of the Chief Factory Inspector has provided more information. The Health and Safety Commission is now expected to remedy this serious lack of information and it is to be hoped that statistics at least as good as those of the National Coal Board and Mines Inspectorate will begin to be given for all industries. Sources of pollution and other threats to the environment have in the past been exposed by the journal *Social Audit* (9 Poland Street, London W1). Major studies have been made of Coalite and Chemical Products, the Avon Rubber Company, Tube Investments and Alkali Inspectorate. From the same address you may obtain the publications of Counter Information Services whose studies have covered, for example, Rio Tinto Zinc, Lucas, Unilever, British Leyland, Courtaulds, GEC, Consolidated Goldfields, the oil companies, property and insurance companies.

INVESTMENT INTENTIONS

How does your company fit in with its industry's investment needs and with other companies' plans? We looked at the TUC checklist for trade unionists to answer in Chapter 11. The Department of Industry publishes a survey made three times a year of industry's investment intentions, and the CBI makes a more detailed survey once a month which is published in the *Financial Times* in full and in summary form in other papers. These give only the broadest picture which you can supplement from the quarterly capital expenditure figures in *Trade and Industry*. You will also find a regional breakdown in *Trade and Industry* and you should make contact with the Regional Economic Planning Board for regional information. There are trade union representatives on the Board who have access to research facilities for studying local investment plans.

ECONOMIC PLANNING

Apart from local and regional studies, you may wish to explore the place your company occupies in the national economy. If you work in a nationalized industry, the Annual Reports of the board or authority will discuss these problems and you can refer to the invaluable evidence presented regularly in relation to each industry to the Select Committee of the House of Commons on the Nationalized Industries. Until more is revealed under the new planning agreements, in the private sector your source must be the National Economic Development Office (Vickers House, Millbank, London SW1). NEDO and the little 'Neddies' for each industry have published a number of studies on the condition and prospects of particular industries and you should be able to find yours among them. Both *Economic Trends* and *Trade and Industry* also publish from time to time reviews of the progress of certain industries and you should look out for those which affect you. Once again make use of your own union's research staff and of the Labour Research Department (38 Blackfriars Road, London SE1) or the Trade Union Research Unit, Ruskin College, Oxford, to either or both of which your union may be affiliated.

13. Following the Financial Analysts

Unless you decide to put the branch funds into stocks and shares (and of course many unions do hold their funds in company securities), you will not be following the City columns of the national press with the aim of making money. But if you wish to build up your own information service, or, more modestly, keep a check on what's happening to your company or industry, you're going to have to follow the financial news. There are three main ways of doing this:

1. Through the newsletters issued by some stockbrokers like Philips and Drew or Hoare & Co., Govett;
2. Through information-collecting agencies like Exchange and Telegraph (EXTEL) Services or Incomes Data Services;
3. Through the bank *Reviews*: Lloyds, National Westminster, Three Banks, Barclays and Barclays DCO, and the National Institute *Review*;

4. Through the so-called 'City' columns: the industrial and commercial, economic and financial columns of the more expensive daily and Sunday papers and the weekly *Economist*.

Once again your own union or the Trade Union Research Unit and the Labour Research Department can help you.

Stockbrokers' Newsletters

These are not so easy to get hold of if you are not a client; but they are often referred to in the City columns and by the Research Units. Look out for what they say. They are often well ahead of the news you can get from the official statistics, since the job of the Stock Exchange is to discount future trends whether they are expected to be upward or downward. Share prices may seem to go up and down with every whisper or rumour or judder of the £ – and they do actually fluctuate like that – but the underlying 'tone', as it is called, depends on expectations of what will happen in the next six months or year. You will need to go to the *Stock Exchange Yearbook*, which will be in your public library, to find out more details about the company you wish to study: its directors, main products, past history, etc. To check on subsidiaries, you can look at *Who Owns Whom*. This should be available in a large public library too.

Agency Services

EXTEL supplies regularly updated comparable information about individual companies which are quoted on the Stock Exchanges. There are separate EXTEL services for London, New York and European quotations, and a fourth covers unquoted British companies. EXTEL (37–45 Paul Street, London EC2) publishes an annual card for each company in its British Company Service. These cards are updated by a news card roughly every quarter. You should ask the librarian at your library (if it is a big one) where to find them and how to use them. You can be sure that he (or she) will be delighted to help you. When we examined the story of the closure of Imperial Typewriters in Chapter 8, we looked at an EXTEL card for Litton Industries. Look back at the illustration now. This one came from their American Service which comes in a folder with a definition of terms used inside the back cover. The British Service of EXTEL gives roughly the same information as on the American card, but by using several cards or two sides of the card there is room for much more detail about the company, its products, financial history, directors' interests, subsidiary companies and a summary of the chairman's latest statement. The American Service, on one side of a card, is in strictly comparable format for each company; at first sight it appears to be extraordinarily complex. The ten-year run of figures is given in $ millions and per share, with other financial ratios worked out for you. Quarterly figures of sales and earnings are given over a five-year period and there are graphs of quarterly movements of earnings, sales, book values, and cash flow per share as well as of share prices. There is a fairly full statement of recent developments and prospects as well as performance and safety gradings. Altogether these cards are invaluable documents and well worth copying from for future use.

Incomes Data Services is included here although it is not a financial analysis, but just what it is called: an incomes data service. It is available (at a reduced rate to WEA districts, among others) from 140 Great Portland Street, London W1. You will find in its bi-monthly reports, studies and briefs all the information you could possibly want about wages, salaries, hours, overtime, and so on, in different firms, occupations and industries, with special studies of new labour legislation, legal cases, redundancies, dismissals; everything for the trade unionist involved in industrial relations. And it now carries a really cheap regular international report (£20 a year in 1976).

The Bank *Reviews* and the National Institute *Review*

The bank *Reviews*, of Lloyds, National Westminster, Three Banks and Barclays and Barclays DCO, especially (now that Hill Samuel's *Moorgate and Wall Street Review* has been closed down), publish articles by distinguished economists and others on key economic and financial issues written in language a layman can understand and often portending important scholarly works that are to follow.

Barclays provides an international view of trading conditions and commodity production and prices throughout the whole world. Apart from their intrinsic merit these reviews are specially attractive because they are issued free!

Here are the addresses:

Lloyds Bank Review, 71 Lombard Street, London EC3;
National Westminster Bank Review, 14 Moorgate, London EC2;
Three Banks Review, 20 Birchin Lane, London EC3;
Barclays Bank Review and *Barclays International Review,* 54 Lombard Street, London EC3.

Besides the bank *Reviews* there is one other invaluable source of analysis and information. This is the National Institute of Economic and Social Research *Economic Review*. It is published quarterly and makes its own forecasts of British economic activity which act as a valuable check on the Treasury's predictions. Apart from the regular review and forecast for the home economy and world economy, it carries articles on specific industries, foreign trade movements, inflation, investment and government economic policies; and its diaries and statistical appendices provide the most useful summaries of all the main economic and financial developments (£10 a year in 1976 from 2 Dean Trench Street, Smith Square, London SW1).

The City Columns

If you don't normally read the 'heavies' of the national press, even to pick them up is a bit of a shock since they really are heavy; but most of the space is occupied by advertisements. So it's only the weight of the rather heavy writing that has to be overcome. *The Times*, the *Guardian*, the *Daily Telegraph*, the *Observer* and the *Sunday Times* all have business and investment sections. The *Financial Times* is almost entirely concerned with such matters, although in fact its arts correspondents are most distinguished. It contains the most reliable trade union news of any newspaper bar none.

The heavies are not to be read from cover to cover. You should just look out for articles of special interest to you, for company news and industry and trade union views that affect you particularly. You will soon get to know the prejudices of different writers: Sam Brittan really doesn't like Labour's interference with the workings of the capitalist system, Joe Rogaly doesn't like trade unions, Gordon Richardson has a sneaking sympathy for the Tribunites. And incidentally, Ken Fleet of the *Daily Telegraph* is not the same as Ken Fleet, the secretary of the Institute for Workers Control.

What you will mainly be looking for in the City columns is up-to-date news of Government statistical series on wages and prices, imports and exports, unemployment rates, capital spending and investment intentions. And of course you can follow day by day the share prices of your company and of other companies you are interested in. It may also be important for you to follow commodity price movements of essential raw materials in your line of business and the sterling exchange rate against other currencies. You should begin by buying a heavy Sunday paper before lashing out on the serious dailies. Once you get the habit of reading the City columns daily, those sessions at the beginning of each day's work will get longer and longer. But no matter, you're learning all the time; and your mates will benefit.

Part IV: How to Talk the Language

Glossary

The definitions of the words that follow are those appropriate to the context of a book about economics and accounting. The same words have different meanings in other contexts; and that is why a Glossary is included in this book with references to it throughout the text.

Account, profit and loss Account giving details of company revenue and expenditure over a financial year.

Accounting period The period of time between the dates of two balance sheets.

Accounts Show the financial state of a business or company at any time or over a particular period, such as a year.

Accounts, consolidated For instance, profit and loss accounts, balance sheets, the accounts of a group of companies required by British company law to be shown separately from the parent company accounts.

Accumulation Increasing sums of money as capital for investment. *See also* Capital; Investment.

Acquisition Purchase by one company of shares in another company or other companies.

Affiliate, associate A person or company working jointly with another person or company in an economic enterprise but not as parent and subsidiary. *See also* Company, parent; Company, subsidiary.

Allowances On personal or company incomes, those costs, such as capital costs or parts of income, which are not subject to tax.

Analysis Breaking down general statements into separate parts, as for example in financial analysis, to reveal basic trends and relations.

Appreciation The increase in value of capital, stocks, etc., through price increases.

Articles of association Regulations governing the internal affairs of a company.

Asset Any property which has a money value, for instance cash, capital, fixed assets like equipment, machinery, buildings. *See also* Cash.

Asset, capital An asset which cannot easily be turned into cash, such as fixed assets, investments in other companies, goodwill. *See also* Goodwill.

Asset, current An asset in the form of cash or easily turned into cash, such as debtors, stocks, short-term loans.

Asset, fixed An asset acquired for using and not re-selling, such as land, buildings, plant, equipment, transport.

Asset, monetary Cash and debtors of a company *less* creditors and excluding stocks.

Asset, net Asset after deducting for depreciation.

Asset stripping Sales of a company's assets to make a money profit whatever the effect on future employment.
Asset, tangible Any asset paid for in taking over a company except items of goodwill, in excess of asset values. *See also* Goodwill.
Associate *See* Affiliate.
Audit Review by an accountant or other independent person, called an auditor, employed to examine accounts and judge whether they reveal the true state of affairs. *See also* Social audit.

Balance For instance of input and output or of imports and exports, the weight of one such category compared with another, generally in money terms.
Balance sheet Statement in a company's accounts at any given time of assets, liabilities and shareholders' funds.
Bank A company (often referred to as an institution) which accepts deposits of money at one rate of interest and lends money at a higher rate of interest, making a profit in the process. *See also* Deposit.
Bank, central In England the Bank of England, the Government's banker.
Bank, clearing A bank which deals directly with the public, such as Lloyds, Barclay.
Bank, commercial Public banking company, for example, Lloyds, Barclay, which, because it is a public company, is often referred to as a joint stock company. *See also* Company, public; Joint stock company.
Bank, merchant Generally a private bank whose customers are mainly other companies or trusts. *See also* Trust.
Bank rate The rate of interest at which the Bank of England will lend to commercial concerns.
Bankruptcy Inability of a person or company to pay debts when called on by creditors to do so.
Benefit Economic advantage.
Bill Trade bill, bill of exchange are terms referring to a claim on a company or person for payment now or at a certain date in the future.
Board as of directors: those people responsible to the shareholders for managing a company.
Bonus Issue *See* Issue, bonus.
Boom Rapid period of growth of output of an economy or several economies. *See also* Slump.
Budget Estimate of receipts and expenditures, for instance by a company or government over a forthcoming period of time, such as a year.
Building society Company that borrows money in order to lend it (at a higher rate of interest, plus repayments) to people who want to build or buy houses and other buildings; it generally retains rights of ownership until payments are complete.

Capacity What a container will hold; therefore, by extension, what can be produced by a plant or machine in a given time.
Capacity utilization Proportion of full capacity at which a plant is operated.
Capital Sum of money invested with a view to obtaining a return in excess of the original sum. *See also* Asset, capital; Equipment, capital; Expenditure, capital.
Capital, risk or ordinary *See* Equity.
Capital structure The make-up of a company's sources of funds, mainly long-term. *See also* Gearing.
Capital, working Current assets less current liabilities. *See also* Asset, monetary.
Capitalism The mode of production in which ownership of capital and the return on capital determine the

allocation of resources and the distribution of income.

Cash Money available for spending.

Cash flow Sums of money coming into and going out of a company at any time, leaving a net profit before charging depreciation, unless the company is bankrupt.

Cash flow, discounted The present value of future receipts and payments of cash, assuming a chosen rate of interest on money borrowed or lent over the period; a calculation used for estimating the return on capital invested in particular projects.

Commodity Anything bought and sold in the market but especially used as a term to refer to raw materials, so-called primary commodities. *See also* Market.

Companies House Office (in London and Cardiff, UK), where all companies must register and public companies must file their accounts, etc.

Company An association of shareholders in a stock of capital which they own but assign to a particular undertaking. The aim is to make a profit (unless the company is designed to be non-profit making). *See also* Capital; Shareholder; Stock; Stock Exchange.

Company, holding Company controlling one or more other companies as subsidiaries, whose shares must be shown separately in the accounts.

Company, limited In this the shareholders' obligations are limited to the capital they have subscribed.

Company, multinational One that draws capital from several countries. Term often used interchangeably with 'trans-national company' (*see below*).

Company, parent The ultimate owner of one or more subsidiary companies in a group of subsidiary or associated companies.

Company, private. One having only the shares of the original subscribers or not more than fifty shareholders.

Company, public One having any number of shareholders and shares that the public can buy and sell.

Company, quoted One having its shares quoted on the Stock Exchange.

Company Report, Accounts The annual survey of the financial position.

Company, subsidiary A company directly owned (at least more than 50 per cent) by another parent company.

Company, trans-national One that has plants or subsidiaries operating in several countries.

Competition, competitors More than one or two companies producing similar goods or services in the market. *See also* Market.

Conglomerate Company with diversified interests in different activities, for instance, finance, insurance, or in companies concerned with the production of many different items.

Consolidated accounts *See* Accounts, consolidated.

Conversion costs Costs of the production process; in effect, the value added. *See also* Value added.

Cooperative Society or company in which the workers own or control the shares in the capital.

Corporation American name for a company, often used by large British companies and nationalized industries (public corporations).

Corporation tax Tax on the income of companies.

Cost Expenditure of money on current and capital items involved in any economic activity.

Cost, bought-in One incurred by purchases outside a company, such as for materials, sub-contractors.

Cost, capital The cost of fixed assets required to produce goods and services, often measured per unit of output.

Cost, current The cost of wages, materials, power, depreciation, overheads, etc., involved in the process of production of goods and services; often called running costs.
Cost, direct *See* Labour cost, direct.
Cost, historic The usual basis of valuation of fixed assets, the actual cost of plant and equipment at the time it was bought; compare with replacement cost.
Cost, indirect *See* Labour cost, indirect; Overheads.
Cost, replacement The actual money cost of replacing plant and equipment; compare with historic cost.
Cost, running *See* Cost, current.
Cost, social Cost borne by society as a whole and not by an individual or company.
Credit Arrangement whereby a buyer may obtain goods or services now and pay later.
Credit guarantee The promise of a government or other third party to underwrite provision of goods or funds on credit. *See also* Underwrite.
Creditor Person or company owed money by another person or company; in accounts refers to the sum owed.
Currency Money that is accepted in any one country as a means of exchange, such as sterling in the UK, dollars in the USA. *See also* Exchange.
Current Adjective meaning what is spent or used up in the present time or short-term future.
Current cost accounting (CCA), Current purchasing power accounting (CCP) Different ways of adjusting current costs of assets for inflationary increases in price over an accounting period.
Current ratio *See* Ratio, current.
Cycle Movement of output, unemployment, etc., showing regular increases and declines over certain periods of time (adjective: cyclical).

Data Pieces of information.
Data processing Arrangement of pieces of information, for instance for a computer to analyse so that the relationships between them can be understood.
Debenture Loan of money, generally tied to a claim on a particular plant, building, or other asset which ranks before other creditors for repayment on the winding up of a company.
Debt Sum of money owed for goods or services purchased and not paid for; or an outstanding loan.
Debt, bad Debt that is written off because it is not expected to be paid. *See also* Loan; Writing off.
Debtor Person or company owing payment; in accounts refers to sums they owe.
Deeds Legal document giving title of ownership, such as of a house.
Deferred taxation *See* Taxation, deferred.
Deficit Negative balance or loss, for instance on a country's foreign payments or a company's cash flow.
Deflator Adjustment of values, for example, of stocks, to take account of price increases.
Deposit Sum of money left in bank, which cannot be withdrawn immediately (that is, without a week's notice), and on which interest is paid by the bank to the depositor.
Depreciation Expense recording the decline in the value of any fixed assets, for instance a car or machine, over the period during which it is expected to be used.
Depreciation provision Annual payments made into a fund to replace an asset at the end of its useful life.
Direct cost *See* Labour cost, direct; Overheads.
Direct labour cost *See* Labour cost, direct.

Director A person elected by the owners of a company or corporation to manage it. *See also* Emoluments; Report, directors'.
Discount Reduction of a sum of money, for example for cash payment. *See also* Cash flow, discounted; Value, discounted.
Disposition In accounting statements about company funds, how money is disposed of in different ways.
Distribution Of profits, the dividend payments made to shareholders; of income and wealth, the proportion of persons having certain levels of income or wealth; of goods, the activities involved in wholesaling and retailing.
Dividend Part of profit distributed to a company's shareholders at a certain rate per share over a period such as a year.
Dividend, final Dividend paid after accounts are drawn up. What is proposed to shareholders must be shown in the accounts as a current liability. The company must deduct personal tax at the standard rate. *See also* Liability, current.
Dividend, interim Dividend paid during year.
Dividend yield Relationship between the ordinary dividend and the market price for an ordinary share.

Earnings Sums of money due as payment for work, or from company activities, or from investment of capital. Earning per share is the net profit after tax attributable to a company's ordinary shareholders, divided by the number of shares. *See also* Capital.
Earnings, gross The amount of money earned by a person or company before tax or depreciation is deducted.
Earnings, net Gross earnings after deduction of tax and depreciation.
Emoluments Payments, for instance to directors for services.
Equipment, capital Machinery, etc., used in the productive process. *See also* Process of production.
Equity Share capital: the name for shareholders' company ownership, that is, the risk or ordinary capital carrying unlimited rights to shares in company profits.
Equity interest That part of the profit which can be claimed by ordinary shareholders.
Exchange Transactions of commodities of equal value, for instance national currencies. *See also* Currency.
Exchange rate Price of any one currency in terms of any other currency.
Expenditure Payment of money from personal or company funds.
Expenditure, capital Payments on fixed assets, for example for plant, buildings, roads and vehicles for economic use.
Expenditure, current Payment for goods, assets, services which will be used up in the near future.
Exports Goods or services supplied to another country.
Extel Exchange Telegraph Service: provides financial information to subscribers.

Fees Charges of persons who are not direct employees of a company, e.g. consultants, auditors, etc., or the employers themselves.
Finance In economics and accounting, the provision of money to a company or other body for its operations; provision of money for specific purposes, for instance depreciation. *See also* Depreciation.
Finance company, house One that provides money for companies and individuals at a rate of interest, against specific purchases, such as of cars or machinery.

Flow, cash *See* Cash flow.
Flow, product *See* Product flow.
Fund, sinking Money set aside each year for repayment of capital as well as interest on certain kinds of loan.
Funds Money that is made available, for instance by shareholders, for business activities or government spending.
Funds, liquid Money immediately available as cash, that is, current assets of a company less stock. *See also* Asset, current.

Gearing Of capital, the ratio of fixed interest charges on it to the shareholders' funds.
Gestation The period between planning the production of goods or services and obtaining payments from sales.
Goodwill A company's order book, or other non-tangible assets, as when taken over by another company, for which a value is placed in the accounts over and above the tangible capital and current assets less liabilities.
Grant Provision of finance, generally by governments for special purposes such as investment, for which no interest is charged.
Gross Of goods or earnings, the bulk before breaking down. *See also* Earnings, gross; Net; Wholesale.
Guarantee Promise to pay a third party's debts up to a certain credit limit.
Guarantor Person, company or government that makes guarantees.

Historic cost *See* Cost, historic.
Holding, beneficial One that gives one company a claim (sometimes control) over another.
Holding company *See* Company, holding.

Import Any goods or services obtained from another country.
Import penetration Proportion of sales of any goods or services in the home market accounted for by imports.
Imputed rent *See* Rent, imputed.
Incidence For instance of taxes: how they affect households of different compositions with different incomes.
Income Moneys received by persons or companies from all sources.
Income, current Income from activities during current accounting period.
Income, gross Income before providing for tax and depreciation.
Income, net Income after providing for tax and depreciation.
Income tax Tax on person's and not company income.
Incorporation Act of establishing and registering a company or corporation.
Index, indices Value, values measured in percentage increases or decreases based on the number 100, over a period of time, such as months, quarters, years, etc.
Index of Retail Prices Index of average prices of goods and services making up the expenditure of an average household.
Indirect cost *See* Labour cost, indirect; Overheads.
Indirect labour *See* Labour cost, indirect.
Inflation Fairly continuous rising prices in an economy.
Information system Collection and analysis of facts and figures to reveal what is happening in an organization such as a company, at any time; often computerized.
Inland Revenue Tax authority in the UK whose job is to collect tax on earnings.
Input As of materials, power, fuel, labour, machine time, etc., put into production processes over a period of time; may be measured in money values or physical quantities.

Institution Insurance company, unit trust, pension fund, bank, being able to hold shares in companies.
Insurance Payment of money (so-called premium) to companies specializing in making provision against illness, death, damage, theft, losses, etc.
Insurance company, house One which specializes in the above provisions.
Interest Payment by a borrower to a lender for use of money.
Interest, rate of Percentage of the sum lent that is charged by the lender, for example, the bank rate.
Inventory In business, list of all items in stock, all plant in use, etc.
Investment In economies, expenditure on fixed assets; in accounting, any placing of money in a bank, building society, company, government or local government stock, for the purpose of making more money.
Investment goods Capital equipment. *See* Equipment, capital.
Issue Offer and taking up of shares in the capital of a company.
Issue, bonus Issue of free shares to shareholders.
Issue price Price at which the share is issued; it may be above or below par value. *See* Value, par.
Issue, rights *See* Rights, issue.
Issue, scrip American word for bonus issue.

Joint stock company Any company of shareholders pooling their funds for some commercial activity; historically used to refer to public companies, particularly banks.

Labour cost, direct Cost of labour applied to productive processes.
Labour cost, indirect Cost of labour applied to administrative, marketing activities, etc.
Labour, division of Way in which work processes are divided up into different tasks which are generally related to the design of machinery.
Labour turnover *See* Turnover, labour.
Lease, leasing Long-term contract to rent land, building or equipment, generally not shown in balance sheet.
Leverage American word for gearing. *See* Gearing.
Liability Sum owed by a company both on capital account and current account, including share capital, which would all have to be paid up on liquidation.
Liability, current One expected to be paid off within one year of the date of its appearance in a company balance sheet as for example, to creditors, taxation, dividends.
Liability, limited *See* Company, limited.
Liquid funds *See* Funds, liquid.
Liquidate To change assets into liquid funds.
Liquidation Voluntary or involuntary bankruptcy or liquidating of a company.
Liquidator Official appointed to sell off the assets of a bankrupt company.
Liquidity Proportion of a person's or company's assets held in liquid form.
Loan Sum of money lent, for example by a bank, which must be repaid according to the terms of the loan; generally not for a short term. *See* Overdraft.
Loan, secured Loan tied to a company asset.
Loan, unsecured Loan not tied to a company asset.
Loss leader Reduction by a company of the price of one popular commodity below cost, so as to encourage purchases of other products on which profits can be made.

Market Any place where goods and services or labour, land and capital are bought and sold; and by extension any situation where these are bought and sold.

Market price, value Actual sum at which sales and purchases are made, including for example VAT and other taxes or the price at which a company's securities can be bought or sold. *See* Value Added Tax (VAT).
Merchant One who lives by buying and selling.
Merchant bank *See* Bank, merchant.
Merger Agreement between two or more companies to join together their capital and operations. *See* Takeover.
Minimum Lending Rate *See* Bank rate.
Minority interest That part of a subsidiary company's shares that are not held by the holding company.
Monopoly A situation where there is one seller of a product or service. A company said to be holding a monopoly position is the only seller in a particular situation or of a particular product.
Mortgage Literally, a promise to the death, generally involving handing over the title to a property (such as the deeds of a house) in order to borrow money. *See also* Deeds.
Multiple activity chart Plan of work, as in a factory, office or mine, showing what each individual worker would be doing at any given time of day.

Net Of income, wealth, payment, assets: after deductions have been made, such as taxes, debts, depreciation, bought-in costs, etc.
Net worth Assets of a company less liabilities.
Nominal value *See* Value, nominal.
Nominee Person or institution, such as a bank, nominated by a shareholder to act on his/her behalf so as to conceal his/her identity.
Norm In industry, the usual and accepted performance of a machine or worker over a given period of time.
Operating Adjective used to describe expenses or profit derived from a company's activities over a period.
Ordinary share *See* Share, ordinary.
Organization tree A chart of an organization; it looks like a Christmas tree or family tree, with the founder or boss at the top and all the different branches spreading out, each descending from and responsible to the one above.
Output The sales, or sales plus stock of products, resulting from production processes over a period of time; may be measured in values or volumes after discounting price increases.
Output, net Output after deducting the value of bought-in costs; is the same as value added.
Overdraft Money borrowed from the bank for a fixed term, generally short term, and up to a certain limit.
Overheads Those costs of a company which continue whether any goods or services are being produced or not, for example, rent, interest, administration.

Partnership Association of persons in a business, each of whom is liable for partnership debts. The liability is unlimited except in the case of limited partnerships.
Patent Government authority imposing a restriction without payment for a licence on the use of an invention that has been described and publicly registered.
PAYE Stands for Pay As You Earn. Income tax deducted by an employer according to codes calculated by the Inland Revenue.
Payroll The total payments of a company to its employees: wages, salaries, National Insurance, fringe benefits.
Performance indicator or ratio One of many ratios used in accounts. *See also* Ratio, current, quick.

Planning agreement Voluntary arrangement under the 1975 Industry Act between government and large companies regarding future investment, employment and pricing policies.
Portfolio Holding by a person, company or government of shares in a number of different companies, excluding direct company investment in subsidiaries.
Preference share *See* Share, preference.
Premium Special price or payment, for instance for an insurance policy or on top of other income or for purchase of shares when issue price is above their nominal value. Share premium reserve in company accounts relates to shares issued above their nominal value.
Price Money measure of value of goods, services, labour, land, capital, etc.
Price control Measures (usually of government) to limit companies' price changes.
Price earnings ratio Current market price of company shares compared with latest company earnings.
Price leadership Determination of prices of goods and services by a very large producer.
Price, transfer Price charged for movements of goods and services between different parts of a large company.
Private company *See* Company, private.
Process of production In industry, a process involving an economic activity in which output can be generated.
Product Result of economic activity in the form of goods or services.
Product, finished, final Product ready to go to consumer.
Product flow Planning of the different stages in the production process so that there are no delays at any stage.
Product, intermediate Product before going to a finishing process.
Product, primary Food or raw materials requiring further processing.
Productivity Measure of value or volume of output per man or per man-hour.
Profit What is received in revenue by a company or self-employed person after paying all costs including interest, rates, rent, etc. *See also* Account, profit and loss; Surplus.
Profit, gross Profit made before providing for depreciation, interest, taxes, fees, etc.
Profit, net Profit after the same provisions have been made.
Profit, pre-tax Profit after providing for depreciation but before paying tax.
Profit, post-tax Profit after providing for depreciation and tax.
Profit, retained That part of company profit kept inside the business for new investment and not distributed to shareholders. Also called retention of profit.
Profit, trading Profit on sales only and excluding income from investments, rent, etc.
Profitability Ability (of a company) to make a profit.
Provision Sums written off capital assets or retained for such writing-off, to provide for depreciation, total write-off, or other losses.
Proxy Person appointed to attend and vote on behalf of a shareholder at a company meeting. Also, the form that grants this authority.
Public company *See* Company, public.

Quotation Of stocks and shares, where permission has been given by a recognized Stock Exchange for dealings to take place in such stocks and shares.
Quoted share *See* Share (or stock), quoted.

Rates Annual payments to local government authorities on the annual value of property, buildings. *See also* Interest, rate of.
Ratio, current Relation of current assets to current liabilities.
Ratio, quick A ratio in which current ratio excludes stock from current assets.
Rationalization Reduction of a company's operations to those plants that are most profitable.
Real For instance, real capital, real cost, real wages: adjective describing the value after allowing for price changes.
Redemption Act of repaying borrowings, shares, etc.
Redemption date Date on which repayment is to be made.
Remuneration Any payment for work or services rendered, including wages, salaries, emoluments. *See* Salary; Emoluments.
Rent Payment for use of land or housing.
Rent, imputed Payment of rent that would have been made if the land or house had not been owned.
Replacement cost *See* Cost, replacement.
Report, company *See* Company Report.
Report, directors' Annual report by the directors of a company that must, under the terms of the Companies Act, include certain details of the company's activities.
Research and development Term used for costs of production not yet realized in the value of goods sold.
Reserves Sums of money arising in company accounts from either retained profits, or issue of shares at a premium, or revaluation of assets. Must be disclosed in the accounts, but are not necessarily available for dividend. *See also* Asset; Premium; Profit.
Retail Sale of goods or services to *final* customers.
Retail price Price of retail sale. *See also* Index of Retail Prices.
Retentions *See* Profit, retained.
Revaluation Writing up of fixed assets to current market value.
Revenue Receipts of money over a period of time. *See also* Inland Revenue.
Rights issue Issue of shares in which the existing shareholders have a right to subscribe at a certain price, generally below market price.
Running cost *See* Cost, current.

Salary Payment to worker at an annual rate, in weekly or monthly instalments, whether he or she is at work or not.
Sales Disposal of goods or services, such as of a company, for money, over a period of time.
Sales value Value of goods or services when sold, that is, covering costs and profit margin.
Savings Income that is not spent in a given period but set aside for future spending.
Scrip issue *See* Issue, scrip.
Seasonal Adjective referring to adjustments of order books, unemployment, prices, etc., to take account of normal changes in the seasonal pattern of events.
Security General word for all claims on property, including company shares, Government stock or other investment. Also, description of any other asset, for example, deeds of a house, which are regarded by banks as backing for borrowing, overdrafts, etc.
Services Economic activity without a tangible product which can be bought and sold, e.g. hairdressing, teaching, nursing.
Share Claim of shareholder to part ownership in a company's capital, or to receipt of dividends from company's profits.
Share capital That part of a com-

pany's capital that has been issued in the form of shares, therefore excludes long-term loans.

Share, issued A share authorized for issue that is actually issued to make up a company's capital.

Share option Title to subscribe for shares at some future date, often at a premium.

Share, ordinary One entitling the owner to share in profits of a company after payment of interest on debentures and preference dividends. *See* Equity.

Share, preference A person holding a preference share is entitled to a fixed rate of dividend before a dividend is paid on ordinary shares and to priority of repayment on winding up a company.

Share (or stock), quoted Share dealt in on the Stock Exchange.

Share (or stock), unquoted Share not dealt in on the Stock Exchange, for instance of private companies.

Shareholder Any person having a claim to part ownership in a company's capital. *See* Share.

Shareholders' funds Funds to which the proprietors have a claim; include capital and reserves.

Slump Decline in output of an economy (or group of economies) over a certain period. *See also* Boom.

Social audit Review of the social costs and benefits of any economic activity.

Speculation Purchase, for instance, of goods, fuel, raw materials, company shares, foreign currency, gold, for the purpose of selling at a profit; generally some risk is involved.

Stagnation A state of no growth in output of an economy (or group of economies) over a certain period.

Stock Raw materials, fuels, work in progress, finished goods held by any company, business, organization.

Stock appreciation Rise in value of stock.

Stock, capital Share in the ownership of companies or in government borrowing.

Stock Exchange Market in which shares in companies or in government stock can be bought and sold.

Stock records Accounts showing the entry and exit of stock.

Stocktaking Annual accounting of value of stocks in hand.

Subsidiary *See* Company, subsidiary.

Subsidy Payment, generally by government, to cover a part of the cost to the consumer, for instance of houses, bread, etc.

Subsidy, cross Carrying of non-profitable plants and activities in a company by other profitable parts, to provide a complete service or keep out competitors.

Surplus Difference between sales value and all costs of production, including those necessary to the actual productive process and attendant transport, etc. (Marxists include in the term 'surplus' all expenditure on selling etc., plus depreciation charges, rent, interest and profits.) *See also* Sales value.

Takeover Purchase by one company or group of more than 50 per cent of another company's capital.

Takeover bid Offer to purchase share capital.

Tax, taxation Government imposts on personal and company income.

Tax, Value Added *See* Value Added Tax.

Taxation, deferred Sums that may be set aside in company accounts for tax payments at a later date.

Trade Buying and selling of goods inside a country; in foreign trade, between countries.

Trade investment Loans and credit provided by a company to its suppliers or customer.

Trademark Distinctive identification of a good or service which pro-

tects it by law from use by others.
Trading activities Term used to describe a company's activities in producing and selling goods and services. Thus, non-trading activities comprise lending and investing to obtain profit other than by trading.
Trading profit Profit from sales of products or services excluding income from investments, rent, etc.
Transfer price *See* Price, transfer.
Trans-national Company *See* Company, multinational, trans-national.
Trust American name for a finance or holding company.
Turnover Sales of a company or business over a particular period, such as a year.
Turnover, labour Entries and departures of employees in a company or industry over a certain period as a proportion of total employment in the company or industry.

Ultra vires Acting beyond its powers, for instance of a company according to its articles of association.
Underwrite To guarantee payment in the event of default, for instance in issue of shares. Underwriter: guarantor of same.
Unit Measure of one of anything, a car, a ton of coal, a pound sterling, a house, a family income.
Unit trust British name for an institution which manages the capital of small investors, placing money in a number of different kinds of shares.
Unquoted share *See* Share (or stock), unquoted.

Value Measure in terms of money of product, output or sales.
Value added That part of the value of output added by the department, division, company or group operations after deducting all bought-in materials and services.
Value Added Tax (VAT) Tax on certain goods according to value added at different stages of production and distribution.
Value, discounted Present value of future cash receipts, taking into account interest that could be earned on cash in hand.
Value, nominal Value of, for example, a share or other capital on the basis of which interest is paid, whatever the price of the share on the market.
Value, par Nominal or face value of a share, not necessarily the same as issue price or market price. *See* Issue price; Market price.
Viability Ability, for instance of a company, to survive and make a profit, or at least avoid bankruptcy (adjective: viable).
Volume As of output or exports, means the change in value deflated for price increases over any period.

Wholesale Sale of goods in bulk before breaking up for retail distribution.
Wholesaler Person who buys in bulk from producers and sells to retailers at a margin of profit. *See also* Profit.
Work in progress Unfinished products included with other stocks in current assets.
Working capital *See* Capital, working.
Worth Value; for instance, net worth is the value of a company's or person's assets after deducting outstanding debts and other liabilities.
Writing down, writing off Process of reducing or cancelling an accounting entry because the debt or asset is of less value or of no value in the market.

Yield For instance on capital, is the income as a percentage of the actual cost of buying a share or stock of capital. *See also* Dividend yield.